INSTRUCTION AND ASSESSMENT OF
ESL LEARNERS

PROMOTING SUCCESS IN YOUR CLASSROOM

INSTRUCTION AND ASSESSMENT OF
ESL LEARNERS
PROMOTING SUCCESS IN YOUR CLASSROOM

FAYE BROWNLIE • CATHERINE FENIAK • VICKI McCARTHY

PORTAGE &
MAIN PRESS

Portage & Main Press acknowledges the financial support of the Government of Canada through the Book Publishing Industry Development Program (BPIDP) for our publishing activities.

Printed and bound in Canada
Book and cover design: Relish Design Studio Ltd.
Cover illustration by Sheryl Wilson, © Neighbourhood Schools' Conference Committee. Used with permission.

05 06 07 08 5 4 3 2

National Library of Canada Cataloguing in Publication

Brownlie, Faye

      Instruction and assessment of ESL learners : promoting success in your classroom / Faye Brownlie, Catherine Feniak, Vicki McCarthy. – 2nd ed.

First ed. published Vancouver : Collaboration Works, cc2000 under title: Promoting success in your classroom : instruction and assessment of ESL learners.

Includes bibliographical references.

ISBN 1-55379-020-0

1. English language – Study and teaching as a second language.
2. English language – Ability testing. I. Feniak, Catherine
II. McCarthy, Vicki III. Brownlie, Faye. Promoting success in your classroom. IV. Title.

PE1128.A2B765 2004   428'.0071   C2004-901709-8

PORTAGE & MAIN PRESS

100-318 McDermot Avenue
Winnipeg, MB
Canada R3A 0A2

Email: books@portageandmainpress.com
Tel.: 204-987-3500
Toll free: 1-800-667-9673
Toll-free fax: 1-866-734-8477

To Kim, Bruce, and Tom for having the stamina needed to withstand our singularly focused, creative energy. We thank you for your support and for your belief in possibilities.

CONTENTS

CHAPTER 7: BEGINNING LANGUAGE LEARNERS AND THEIR PARENTS

PREFACE TO THE SECOND EDITION

Since the first edition of this book was published in 2000, Faye completed her work in Latvia on the Bilingual Education Project with Open Schools. She is currently a co-chair of the International Reading Association Special Interest Group, International Partnerships for Critical Thinking and Active Learning. Catherine and Vicki are both vice-principals with the Vancouver School Board, and Vicki has completed her doctorate in ESL education. The authors continue to be passionate about informed, inclusive education for all learners.

PREFACE TO THE FIRST EDITION

Not so very long ago, Faye and Catherine were facilitating a workshop for elementary and secondary teachers on the topic of their new book, *Student Diversity: Addressing the Needs of All Learners in Inclusive Classroom Communities*. Vicki, then working as an ESL consultant for the Vancouver School District, was at the workshop. At the end of the session she spoke passionately to Faye and Catherine about how important inclusive school communities were relative to the needs of ESL students. "ESL learners need a sense of community and more explicit teaching. In addition, their teachers need an elaboration of these ideas you have been presenting in a book that is specifically about the challenge of teaching increasing numbers of ESL students," she said.

Faye and Catherine queried whether or not such a book had already been written. "No such thing exists," Vicki emphasized. She was completing her doctoral studies in ESL education at the University of British Columbia and was feeling "confidently current" about available materials. "Too often ESL needs are gathered in with those of other students with special needs. We need a book that focuses exclusively on the needs of ESL learners in regular classes."

Soon after this conversation, the three of us asked ourselves, "What does inclusion look like through the eyes of students new to English?" In search of answers, we began organizing our resources and experiences: the recent writing experience and staff development expertise of Faye and Catherine combined with Vicki's recent reading and research.

We have found our collaboration to be exciting. It has refined our thinking and our new beliefs about teaching and learning. We hope that this book fuels your thinking, encourages you to work in a spirit of collaboration with your colleagues, and challenges you to reflect on your practice. Teaching is a responsive activity. We continually challenge ourselves to put into practice the best of what we know as we search for new knowledge for changing contexts.

Good luck and great teaching!

CHAPTER 1

WHERE ARE WE GOING IN ESL EDUCATION?

BEYOND SEPARATE PROGRAMS

Twenty years ago, educators ran separate "new immigrant" classes outside the mainstream of the school for those students learning English as a second language (ESL). ESL learners participated in numerous workbook-type, repetitive exercises and drills of the English language in isolation of curriculum content; the focus was on form, not on meaning. The students seldom interacted in any meaningful way with their age and grade peers.

Despite the isolation, ESL learners were thought to "enrich the culture of the school" merely by being present. Yet, at school these same students were prohibited from speaking in their own languages. To do so, it was thought, would interfere with their learning of English. Often, those who did speak their own languages were punished. Some were inappropriately made to put coins in a piggy bank; others were forced to write lines for failing to speak English "all of the time."

Teachers of English as a second or additional language were also isolated. They worked alone away from the mainstream classroom, either in a separate class or in a "pull-out" situation.

> In earlier decades in the U.S., we emphasized teaching second language as the first step, and postponed the teaching of academics.
>
> Research has shown that postponing or interrupting academic development is likely to promote academic failure in the long term.
>
> —W. Thomas and V. Collier, *School Effectiveness for Language Minority Students*

TOWARD INCLUSION

Today, educators know that ESL learners in K-12 classes cannot afford to spend time learning the English language in isolation of the curriculum content the students must master to be successful at school. ESL learners must continue to develop cognitively and academically while learning the English needed to be successful with the content of science, social studies, mathematics, and other curricula. Postponing, for too long, access to the language needed to master the mainstream curriculum promotes failure. ESL students not only learn the culture of the school, they help create it. The better schooled that ESL learners are in their first languages, the better learners and users of English they become in the long term.

ESL specialists, too, belong in the mainstream classroom where they can monitor student progress. In the classroom, they can also collaboratively plan and model teaching strategies to support the staff development of colleagues so that all teachers in the school work more effectively to ensure the success of all learners, including the ESL learners they teach.

> Exemplary ESL programs incorporate cultural aspects of students' backgrounds into meaningful language learning experiences and apply ESL techniques to content areas taught through English. In English as a subject class, for example, vocabulary and grammatical structures are taught in isolation but in meaningful contexts, relevant to students' learning experiences and to their lives as members of linguistically and culturally diverse communities.
>
> —TESOL, *Bilingual Basics*

EFFECTIVE SCHOOL-BASED PLANNING FOR ESL LEARNERS

Schools that work most effectively with ESL learners share certain qualities and beliefs about teaching and learning. Our beliefs about school-based planning for ESL learners are supported both by what we, as educators, have observed over many years in these schools and by current research in language education.

> This approach, which is also called cooperative, collaborative, parallel, or team teaching, involves the ESL teacher and the mainstream teacher in a close working relationship. The ESL teacher usually works in the mainstream classroom to support the second language development of individual pupils by collaborating with the classroom teacher to develop suitable curriculum approaches…
>
> —M. Ashworth, *Effective Teachers, Effective Schools*

- The most effective way to teach ESL students is neither by "sink or swim" mainstreaming without support nor by "pull-out" instruction. ESL learners are best monitored and supported in classrooms where they have the opportunity for an occasional short-term, one-shot lesson in a specific area that they may find difficult.

- Classroom teachers and ESL teachers benefit from each other's support. In this way, the teachers work together, not side by side on parallel agendas. ESL teachers can model explicit language teaching while classroom teachers model age- and grade-appropriate curriculum content. Both models are necessary in order to provide an effective learning environment. ESL specialists belong in the classroom, collaboratively planning and team teaching to provide the best learning environment for *all* students.

- Learning requires taking risks. The classroom and the school must, therefore, be emotionally safe places for everyone. Teachers need to model for students that "we are in this together, and together we are better." Teasing and other negative behaviors are not tolerated.

> There is little evidence that the isolated teaching of rules and structures has any effect on actual language use. The process of writing should occur in all curriculum areas, not only in the language arts.
>
> —P. Gibbons, *Learning to Learn in a Second Language*

- The goal for ESL students of all ages is to learn the English of the school curricula (that is, science, mathematics, social studies, language arts, history, music), not the English language in isolation of these curricula. There is no specific "ESL curriculum"; the language of the subject curricula *is* the ESL curriculum.

- ESL learners cannot afford to wait several years before being integrated in the mainstream of the school. They need exposure to age-and grade-appropriate content that challenges them intellectually and through which they can acquire English as soon as possible. Schools and teachers need to have high expectations of students who are learning English as a second language; ESL learners must be expected to succeed and be supported in doing so.

- School staff must be interested in and committed to ongoing professional development explicitly designed to serve ESL students more effectively and sensitively. In schools with large numbers of ESL students, every teacher must make their education a priority.

- Schools need to involve families and use translators to offer support. Parents of ESL learners want to be involved in their children's education but often do not know how to go about it. Many lack the English skills needed to communicate at school or to understand aspects of curriculum and instruction, and they are too embarrassed to ask for translators.

- The support services and extracurricular activities of the school need to be designed to include ESL students. Some students require emotional support while they learn how to become involved in school activities, and they need to know who to seek out for help.

- School staff members must recognize and show that they value the various languages and cultures that students bring to school. The school must be positively responsive to diversity. Research shows that the development of students' home languages needs to be encouraged in a variety of ways both inside and outside the classroom to support the learning of English at school.

- There is tremendous variability in the language backgrounds of ESL learners. A student's background greatly influences his/her future learning. Competency in the first language(s) or the language of the home varies from student to student. There will be a range of abilities in the classroom: some students may be able to speak but unable to read and write; others may be more able with pen and paper. Some students will already be speaking more than one language. For others, the acquisition of a second language will be a new experience, and they may be the primary communicator in this language outside the home.

- ESL learners have tremendously different personal histories. Some students may have been born in an English-speaking country (such as Canada or the United States), but do not speak English at home. Others may be new or recent immigrants or refugees. Some may have had extensive schooling in their home country; others may have had little or no formal schooling.

- Teachers need to encourage bilingualism. Students who graduate fluent in two or more languages will contribute greatly to the world of the future. Research shows that students who are fully bilingual are at an advantage: they score higher on verbal and nonverbal intelligence tests, and they are able to move easily between two or more languages and cultures, thinking fluently in both.

EFFECTIVE ELEMENTARY SCHOOLING FOR SECOND-LANGUAGE LEARNERS

Younger learners do not necessarily acquire English faster than older students. As the curriculum increases in difficulty with subject content over time so, too, do the challenges for the ESL learner.

- Schools need to provide more explicit teaching. All learners – primary as well as intermediate and secondary – need explicit teaching. All learners need to respond to information texts as well as to stories.

- ESL learners arrive at school with five or more years of another language. To ensure that they grow cognitively and academically, their home-language development must continue until their English catches up. If not, they will have difficulty with literacy later.

- Students need explicit teaching to learn how to work with text material; that is, how to organize the information they must learn and how to express in different writing forms what they have learned. They also need to know strategies they can apply to other learning and how to seek out additional resources and materials from the library, the World Wide Web, and other places.

In primary classrooms, the following considerations are helpful to teachers in planning for the inclusion of the ESL learners:

- Encourage students to write in pictures or use rebuses.

- Give students lots of time for play, alone and with others.

- Encourage students to use drawings, clay, and mime to communicate.

- Post "survival language" – visual signs – around the classroom and on the desks of ESL students (e.g., recess, washrooms).

- Encourage students to use the different languages in the classroom.

> Studies suggest that it is not valid to assume that students, even those from low socio-economic levels, minority cultures, or non-English-speaking backgrounds, lack basic knowledge of print and its uses, despite what reading readiness or other standardized reading tests may indicate. It is important for teachers to discern the literacy knowledge students have in both English and their primary language and to find ways to draw on and validate this knowledge in their classrooms.
>
> —K. Spangenberg-Urbschat and R. Pritchard, *Kids Come in All Languages*

- Establish routines so students can predict what is going to happen next.

- Invite students to bring in photo albums. They can label the photos, ask and answer simple questions about the pictures, and refer to the photos when they need comfort. Be sensitive to students who have suffered trauma or who have painful memories of the move.

- Have students keep a special toy at their desk.

- Use wordless picture books. Students can use the books to create a story in any language, or they can dictate their story to a scribe.

- When reading with older buddies, try to pair students with another student who shares the same first language. Together, they can read and write in two different languages, English and their home language.

- Be prepared to wait six months to a year for ESL students to develop the English-language skills and confidence they need to participate comfortably in social conversation.

In an intermediate classroom, the following considerations are helpful in planning for the inclusion of ESL students:

- Encourage students to keep a translation dictionary at their desk to assist in finding key words. Some students now use electronic dictionaries for this purpose.

- Encourage ESL learners to draw their ideas or speak in their first language when other students are writing their responses in English. When learners are ready, they can write in their first language or in English.

- Encourage ESL students to respond in their first language while a more fluent English speaker translates. Classroom groupings should change frequently, however, and teachers must be very careful not to "burn out" the translators.

- In groups of three, have students mime idioms and specialized language in the texts being read. This activity helps to solidify the concepts for all students.

- When reading a text that is above the comprehension level of a new ESL student, have the student circle the words he/she knows and also choose two or three new words to learn.

- Encourage new ESL students to keep a sketchbook at their desk. The student draws on one page, and on the opposite page a trusted buddy writes about what he/she sees in the drawing. Alternatively, the buddy can draw in response to what he/she sees in the drawing.

- Have ESL students keep the following in their desk: an easy chapter book in English to read, an easy English content book, a book in their first language for silent reading periods, and a journal for writing in their first language. For some students, it is also appropriate to have a book of maps (unless there has been a trauma associated with the move) and a photo album of "places I have been," family members, and special occasions (unless these are unavailable or are too painful to recall).

- Have the school librarian show beginners where to find easy-to-read age- and grade-appropriate books in English so they can take them out independently.

- Teach students how to work with the individual novel study frame (see chapter 8, pages 94-98). They can use the forms on their own after they have learned how it works. They can respond in words and in sketches to books that they select independently once the librarian has shown them where to find the books.

- Have beginners focus more on writing than on the spelling and editing of written work. Encourage them to write in English, where possible, or in a combination of English and their first language, if needed. Save writing samples in a portfolio so that students can observe their own progress.

- Have beginning ESL students make word banks in various subject areas (e.g., science, social studies). The word bank can contain new words on index cards with English on one side and a home-language reminder on the other. Students can add a few words each day and practice the words with a buddy.

- Have beginners work in cooperative groups where they can learn how activities work from watching their peers.

- Have ESL students and their buddies keep response journals. In the journal, they can write to each other, read to each other, and ask each other questions (orally for beginners and in writing for intermediate and advanced ESL learners).

- Give beginners the answers and/or a correct model from which to work so that they can complete tasks. Remind students that the emphasis is on completing the task (the process of learning and the language and the task), not on making a product for marking.

- Teach how information texts are organized in various subjects. In social studies, for example, time lines and cause-and-effect are frequently used; in science experiments, procedures are sequenced; structure/function diagrams or charts are often used in science texts.

- Have high expectations for the success of ESL students. Challenge them with open-ended activities. Think of them as students first, ESL learners second, and expect them to learn enthusiastically when they are interested in school and learning.

EFFECTIVE SECONDARY SCHOOLING FOR SECOND-LANGUAGE LEARNERS

The dropout rate in secondary grades is much higher for ESL learners whose English language support is discontinued than it is for those who receive support. Schools need to be careful not to misdiagnose learners as being proficient in measures of the English language in isolation of the curriculum content. Students often seem proficient orally, but they do not have the English needed to read and master curriculum content.

- Create "homework help" clubs, using peer tutors and volunteers from the school community, to provide ongoing support both in the classroom and after school.

- Use of the home language at school for learning enhances the learning of the English needed to master the curriculum of the school. Secondary students who are encouraged to use their first language at school for learning are more likely to be motivated to learn and to complete school. Where possible, organize first-language peer support groups.

- Ensure that the cultural and linguistic diversity of ESL students is respected. Create multicultural clubs to provide orientation and support for newcomers.

- Make information in secondary texts more accessible to ESL students. Help the students learn strategies to organize and work with the complex ideas presented in texts. ESL students will benefit from explicit teaching that coordinates the learning of language with the learning of academic subject matter or content. Explicit teaching of how and when to use graphic organizers has been shown to be useful for learning ESL (Mohan 1986; Mohan, Leung, and Davison 2001).

SUPPORTING ESL LEARNERS IN THE MAINSTREAM CLASSROOM SETTING

In mainstream classroom settings, teachers can do several things to support ESL students. Here are some suggestions.

- Talk more clearly by reducing the speed and complexity of the words while continuing to offer challenges.

- Increase repetition and reinforcement of ideas taught.

- Pause frequently, and check for student comprehension. ESL students are adept at learning to locate bits of information in texts and giving factual answers. However, studies show that they often have a marginal understanding of what it is they are copying or memorizing to fill in blanks and respond to factual statements on worksheets.

- Supplement having students locate and repeat information verbatim from texts with activities that require learners to form opinions, and support their ideas by synthesizing information in written form.

- Use concrete objects and experiences to give students a common context for using language in groups; for example, everyone has experienced the same thing in class.

- Balance explicit teacher-led discussions with opportunities for ESL students to talk with their peers about what they are learning.

- Ensure beginners interact with more advanced learners of the language so that all students are challenged and learn from practicing with each other. Studies show that students benefit from teaching or applying their learning to others.

- Teach grammar in meaningful contexts. "Fill-in-the-blank" worksheets are not effective because they teach language in isolation of curriculum content, context, or meaning.

- Supplement textbooks with other reading materials such as magazine articles and newspapers to expose students to a wide variety of sources.

- Use graphic organizers to support the learner's understanding of concepts in English. Graphics help ESL learners organize both their ideas and the written information in texts.

- Scaffold activities. Present information in a step-by-step, concrete, and clear manner.

- Model the tasks ESL students are expected to accomplish before they begin to work on them.

- Give ESL students more time than mainstream students, if needed, to complete tasks. Reduce the number and complexity of the questions ESL learners are expected to complete.

- Build in a variety of opportunities for students to show their learning – verbally, in writing, on tape, in graphic form – through attention to the multiple intelligences of each learner.

- Teach all students how to work effectively in groups so that ESL students new to working in groups learn what is expected of them and all students work as members of a team, supporting each other's learning.

- Help students understand that becoming bilingual is an asset.

- Make directions clearer for ESL students by writing and drawing instructions on the chalkboard in a step-by-step manner and offering individual support, as needed.

CHAPTER 2

COLLABORATION: CLASSROOM TEACHERS AND ESL TEACHERS AS A TEAM

BENEFITS OF COLLABORATION

In the past, it was common for beginning ESL students to be gradually integrated into the mainstream classes of the school, while being pulled out by ESL specialists who provided the necessary ongoing learning support for them. While that model was thought to be effective, it is not as effective as providing support in a language environment that includes proficient speakers of English; that is, in the regular classroom. Where a high proportion of the students are learning to speak English, language and literacy instruction are the focus of the classroom.

In some schools, ESL teachers team with support teachers (such as learning assistance teachers, teachers of the learning disabled, and resource teachers) to form a noncategorical resource "team." Classroom teachers are then assigned one teacher from this team to provide support, and together they work out how best to meet the needs of the students in their classroom. The resource team meets weekly to share expertise and problem-solve challenging situations. An advantage of this model is that a classroom teacher has only *one* support person for all the students in his/her classroom, while each support person's teacher contact is reduced to several classroom teachers (rather than all teachers with only a few students in each class). Collaborative planning with the classroom teacher and the support teacher is now not only plausible, but possible.

In some schools, the ESL teachers collaborate directly with the classroom teachers, without sharing the roles of the other support personnel. The goal is still the same: to provide maximum support for the learners in a rich language environment.

> Instructional methods that reflect current theory have shifted from an emphasis on separate, isolated skills to an integration of listening, speaking, reading, writing and thinking. This shift challenges curriculum writers and teachers to reorganize instruction with new and authentic approaches to language and literacy in mind.
>
> —K. Spangenberg-Urbschat and R. Pritchard, *Kids Come in All Languages*

> The rationale for partnership teaching is that all teachers share responsibility for meeting the needs of ESL students. According to the Peel Region Board of Education in Ontario, a successful collaborative relationship between teachers begins with the recognition that integration is a developing and changing process. The teachers plan together, share experiences, communicate openly, consider each other, value individual teaching and learning styles, appreciate others' expertise and help and support each other.
>
> —M. Ashworth, *Effective Teachers, Effective Schools*

When beginning an ESL/classroom teacher collaboration, remember the following:

- Too often, teaching is a solitary performance without the inclusion of shared professional expertise. With collaboration, each teacher brings expertise to the team, which is critical to the development of all learners, including ESL.* The classroom teacher brings content knowledge, curriculum expertise, and age-appropriate expectations. The ESL teacher brings language-learning expertise and cultural support. All of these areas weave together to create powerful learning environments for students.

- Two heads are better than one. Working together in the classroom strengthens the plans that are made for students. Two teachers are now available for:
  - planning and implementing curriculum lessons
  - providing appropriate, ongoing adaptations as needed by learners
  - reflecting on the success of the instruction, then beginning the planning cycle again

- Students have access to two teachers. This can increase students' time on task and their personal meaning-making of the content of the lesson. Later, when only one teacher is present, students are better able to perform independently, having been coached, when needed, within the context of the lesson.

- *All* students learn from participating with two adults who are modeling the power of working together.

- ESL students learn language *in use* rather than language separated from the content of the curriculum.

- Both the ESL teacher and the classroom teacher assume various roles while working together. For example:
  - One can teach the whole class while the other works in a support role.
  - They can divide the class into two groups and each take one group.
  - One can work with the whole class while the other works with students who require specific skill intervention.

  The roles tend to be fluid and constantly changing, based on the needs of the students.

- Students spend most of their time in the classroom. However, it is still possible to pull out a student or a small group of students for a specific intervention as needed. The important question is, "What do these students need?" not, "Where should the service take place?"

  When ESL students spend most of their time in the regular classroom rather than away for some kind of "mystery programming," the teachers can work together to build emotional and cultural supports for them. "We all belong in this room together" permeates the classroom.

---

* Additional information on this noncatagorical resource model is found in chapter 7 of *Learning in Safe Schools: Creating Classrooms Where All Children Belong*, by F. Brownlie and J. King.

- Assessments become more curriculum based, more ongoing, and less formal. Teachers find themselves engaged in frequent conversations about their students and their progress.

ADAPTING CURRICULUM AND INSTRUCTION FOR THE ESL LEARNER

To support the learning of ESL students in the classroom, teachers must be receptive to adaptation. Most curriculum documents describe the following options for adaptations:

- **format for the resources:** using tape-recorded books and hands-on resources

- **environment:** seating arrangements such as students sitting at tables or in side-by-side desks with both ESL students and non-ESL students, using cooperative groupings and translators

- **method of presentation:** using advance organizers to help students access text, and adjusting the time allotted for activities

- **materials:** using manipulatives, large print, highlighter pens

- **methods of providing assistance:** using peer or adult tutors, school and area resource teachers

- **instructional strategies:** using visuals to help students develop conceptual knowledge by organizing information effectively; explicit, sequential instructions

- **assessment procedures:** providing a variety of ways beyond pencil-and-paper tests for students to demonstrate understanding; for example, tape recording student responses

Additionally, ESL learners need the following adaptations:

- using the language of the home for learning in order to support the learning of English and to feel included at school

- culturally sensitive teaching and ongoing emotional support. It is important to plan for the inclusion of the students' views, ask for information about their homes and countries of origin, and provide positive reinforcement that supports each small step toward mastering a very difficult language – the English of the curriculum.

- peer support and inclusion in the daily extracurricular activities of the peer group at school

- time to process information in English, both verbally and in writing

- explicit teaching in an integrated approach in order to bridge the gap between language and curriculum content. Teachers must teach language with content and mediate between language and content to support the language learner.

TEACHING EFFECTIVELY IN MULTI-LEVEL CLASSES

Most teachers have classes with students of mixed ability and language proficiency. Several strategies work effectively in these kinds of classrooms.

- **Have a whole-class plan with individual adaptations.**

  Have a class plan that is aligned with curriculum objectives. With this plan in mind, organize for whole-group instruction, small-group practice, and individual response. ESL learners and other students with special needs will require adaptations to this plan from time to time. However, rather than design a separate curriculum, it is preferable to adapt one or more of the following:

  - presentation of content

  - time allotted to working with the content

  - materials used to learn the content

  - amount of support provided

  - evaluation techniques used

  - goals or expectations of the learning

  Adaptations to a group plan help to enhance the ESL student's feeling of belonging and support language acquisition tied to the content of the curriculum.

- **Use a strategic planning process.**

  When planning a lesson or unit sequence, follow a framework for supporting learning. Divide the lesson into three segments: *connecting, processing,* and *transforming or personalizing.* In each segment of the lesson, ask yourself: "How will this provide support to students at this time? How much support is needed?" The connecting stage is critical for ESL learners. At this stage, they access the background knowledge that they already have and build additional background knowledge. Without active learning time in the connecting stage, the other stages of the lesson can be lost – new information has no obvious place for connections. The connecting stage is also a critical time for building curiosity and uncovering misconceptions. In the processing stage, new information is linked to old information. This, too, is an active process. Finally, the transforming or personalizing stage is the time for consolidating learning and being prepared to present new learning in a format different from the way it was originally presented. This helps ensure long-term learning.

- **Use cooperative learning.**

  When students are placed in heterogeneous groups, they must negotiate for meaning, learn to give and take, practice extended conversational exchanges, and adopt a variety of roles unique to their situation. Teachers can develop activities – such as jigsaws, problem-solving opportunities, centers, or simulations – where each student has one piece of the puzzle and must work with others and share information to complete the task.

Heterogeneous groups promote learner responsibility and build cross-cultural friendships; each student is responsible for completing some aspect of a task and for supporting other group members.

■ **Present information in varied ways.**

Teachers can reduce the ESL students' need to rely on understanding the language by placing information in a context that is comprehensible to the students. Consider using a variety of intelligences when designing lessons for discovery learning; for example, verbal and kinesthetic. Use inquiry learning to challenge the ESL students in your class. In a science or social studies class, have groups work together to form a hypothesis, design procedures, conduct research, and solve problems. Real questions lead to real learning.

■ **Incorporate peer tutoring.**

When students work well together in class, it leads to a better affective climate in the classroom: quieter ESL students participate, all students learn to cooperate in an effort to complete common goals, and students are more motivated to learn the language to communicate with peers. With peer tutoring, beginning and intermediate ESL learners have the benefit of support, and more proficient learners have a chance to apply what they know. Teaching is the highest level of learning.

■ **Incorporate process writing.**

We learn to write by writing. Beginning writers, both ESL and non-ESL, focus on putting their ideas on paper, not on editing. As writers' proficiency grows, however, teach ESL learners correct forms of English by encouraging them to learn how to edit and proofread their own work. Provide frequent opportunities for writing throughout the day. Students need time to write in reflection of their learning, record new ideas, generate stories and poems, and communicate information. Involvement in Writer's Workshop or in the writing process extends ESL students' writing and thinking skills and supports their development in a highly individualized way.

■ **Build criteria for success with your students.**

All students, including ESL students, perform better when the criteria for success are clear and available. Criteria are standards for performance – the "what counts." Performance is enhanced even more when students are involved in the building of these criteria, based on the work they are doing together. When students negotiate criteria, those criteria are *owned* by the students and *understood* by the students.

CHAPTER 3

COMMONLY ASKED QUESTIONS

Question: Do ESL learners and native-English speakers learn to read and write in English in the same way?

ESL learners bring to school culturally based rules and expectations for language use in various situations. Often, these rules differ from those of the teacher or the school culture. In some cultures, for example, a girl does not speak until she has been given permission to do so by one of the boys in the room. This, as an example, certainly poses a challenge for our very oral classrooms. Reading, too, can be extremely difficult for the ESL learner. Reading is much more than the ability to decode words on a page. To read for understanding, there is a heavy reliance on systems of language and prior experiences to predict meaning. ESL learners make their predictions based on diverse cultural and societal backgrounds.

To support learning to read in English, ESL learners need the following:

- a print-rich language development program with age-appropriate books in English and, if possible, in the languages of the learners, which enables them to continue thinking and reading with age-appropriate text

- opportunities to use print to express themselves in meaningful ways as they learn about the culture of the school

- activities that build on backgrounds, interests, and strengths so they can draw on what they know culturally

- activities that involve real communication rather than worksheets, and authentic language arts experiences that do not rely on oral repetition

- multi-sensory input

- understandable teacher-talk with an appropriate level of complexity

- access to challenging information books and stories that are at an appropriate age and grade level

- encouragement to take risks with the language without fear of failure or humiliation in front of peers; students and teachers have to accept and expect errors

- a sense of accomplishment fostered by having their work displayed

- time: not all students respond at the same time or in the same way

- opportunities to negotiate meaning with others in small groups; ESL learners must be active participants in their own language learning

Question: How is teaching reading to ESL learners different from teaching reading to native-English speakers?

ESL learners develop reading abilities in a similar manner to native-English speakers. However, there are some differences.

- Greater cognitive demands are placed on ESL students, who are developing both oral and reading skills in English at the same time. Fluent English learners already have oral skills in English and a vast and varied English vocabulary from which to draw.

- ESL learners start learning to read in English at a variety of different ages, and they bring to the task diverse educational and language backgrounds, as well as cultural experiences of the world. They have different contexts for learning and for making predictions. Instructional approaches need to be developed on an individual basis because of the many variables brought to the task.

- Discussions of prior knowledge require the teacher to have an understanding of students' backgrounds, home languages, and cultures.

- English learning strategies are more important to assist with comprehension. Strategies learned in another country may not automatically transfer to reading in English. Being aware of the strategies used in comprehending also allows for better monitoring and control by the reader.

- ESL students may be unfamiliar with and have to learn how various genres are organized in English. Literacy for ESL learners needs to involve the use of many different genres, not just simple stories.

- Because ESL learners have many words in other languages and not in English, they need support to learn meanings. Reading needs to be highly contextualized through visuals, demonstrations, and field trips.

- ESL learners may not be familiar with the symbol/sound system. They may not be able to tell whether a "sounded-out" word sounds like English or makes sense. They may not recognize an error, and they may not know how to correct it. They have not yet developed an "ear" for English.

- ESL learners may not be familiar with the words that are carrying key information in English during reading and may not have the background knowledge needed to make predictions. Ongoing support is needed.

Question: How long does it take to learn English as a second language?

The length of time it takes an ESL student to acquire proficiency in English depends upon a number of variables. These include:

- previous experiences with oral and written English

- previous school experiences (academic background, structure and expectations of the school, interrupted schooling, or a lack of formal schooling)

- experiences prior to entry to the current school

- proficiency in the first or home language

- trauma prior to entry to the current school

- motivation to learn English and having support from home for doing so

- training and expertise of teachers

Research from a variety of sources has reached some consensus regarding the length of time it takes to learn English as a second language. ESL students with previous academic schooling and some exposure to English take up to seven years to master the English of the curriculum. For students with interrupted education, trauma, or no previous exposure to English, learning can take longer.

Communicative competence in English is generally described in two different ways (Cummins 1989, 1983):

I. Social communicative competence in the English language.

It takes ESL learners in our schools, on average, from two to three years to develop the English language needed for day-to-day basic communication with peers and teachers – natural speech used in the halls, on the school grounds, in the cafeteria, and in the community. Social language facilitates the development of a healthy social life at school and is important for students.

2. Academic communicative competence in the English language.

Anywhere from five to ten years is needed for an ESL student to acquire the English-language proficiency needed to reach his/her academic potential on par with native-English speakers in the classroom. ESL learners need to acquire proficiency in the English of the curriculum to reach their potential in mathematics, social studies, science, language arts, or other content areas.

Success at school demands that students develop an understanding of the English language associated with thinking processes such as generalizing, inferring, judging, evaluating, or predicting. Success demands that students learn how the language of social studies is related to, but also different from, the language of science or mathematics or the language arts. It demands that students develop the ability to read and write to learn in English in many subject or content areas.

Does the acquisition of academic language require deliberate teaching? Yes! Direct, thoughtful, and very specialized teaching is needed to help ESL students reach their potential academically as they learn to master the curriculum of the school in English.

Question: How do you learn a first and/or a second language?

All language learners

- make gradual approximations toward standard forms of the language over time. Making errors is a natural part of the learning process.

- learn their first language at home, a highly contextualized and supportive environment where attempts at producing language are rewarded and errors are not marked or corrected.

- learn language best in context. Grammar is not learning as an end in and of itself.

- rely heavily on chunks, phrases, or known items in the language. They apply known items to new situations over time.

- rely on content words and phrases for meaning.

Many ESL learners

- encounter English for the first time at school, which is a highly formalized and unnatural environment for learning language.

- feel threatened, frustrated, and anxious about attempting to produce correct forms of the new language. No one wants to be wrong and laughed at.

- benefit from a supportive learning environment where they are encouraged to take risks and make mistakes.

- learn more effectively when their home languages and cultures are respected.

Question: Is acknowledging culture really important in teaching ESL students?

Language learning, whether it is for social or academic purposes, is also cultural learning. ESL students come from another part of the country or the world, and they bring a prior knowledge of school and of how things work socially. They also bring values, beliefs, and norms for learning and living. They have learned a language other than English for at least five years prior to school entry and express their knowledge of the world through this language. For ESL learners to feel safe socially and academically, the cultural diversity that they bring with them to the classroom must be valued. This means:

- showing respect for the first/home languages of the learners. ESL learners should not be punished, made to write lines, or feel that the school wants to eliminate their languages.

- encouraging learners to become bilingual, rather than to replace one language with another. New concepts and ideas learned in English will be integrated with those already known from another social and cultural situation.

- promoting activities that bridge differences and encourage respect for diversity. Have signs and other displays around the school in languages other than English.

- making the classroom and the school safe places by having books and materials in the library in languages other than English.

- incorporating diversity into the curriculum. Discussion about culture should include the culture of the learners. Textbooks must represent the diversity of the learners.

- encouraging learners to contribute ideas and experiences from their diverse backgrounds and building upon these ideas rather than replacing them with new ones.

- ensuring that assessment is free from cultural bias.

There are strong links between learning, achievement, and respect for cultural and linguistic diversity. To show disrespect for the background experiences that language learners bring to school is to inhibit learning. Schools and classrooms must provide caring and effective environments and support activities that foster learning.

CHAPTER 4

ORIENTATION TO SCHOOL

THE FIRST DAYS

There are a number of ways that schools can welcome new ESL students and provide them with a safe environment in which to learn: Posters that welcome students in a variety of languages, culturally inclusive displays and pictures, books in the library in languages other than English, access to translated information about the school, and a video showing a "typical day at school" are welcome sights to new families. It is important for these families to feel that such diversity is a natural part of the school environment. It is equally imperative that the students' parents know that the school values bilingualism and views it as an advantage: their children are not going to lose languages they already know; they are going to learn *another* language.

Teachers can also have resources available that will help students learn about the school. One very effective way to ease ESL students into their new school is through the orientation activity. With its hands-on approach, new students are introduced to the school and its staff in a nonthreatening and interesting manner.

To begin, try to pair each new ESL student with a buddy (or two) who speaks the same first/home language and enough English to complete the task. This pairing will facilitate translation when it is needed and make the activity easier.

Give the students a copy of the orientation activity (see figure 1), and have them complete it as they travel through the school. Students can usually complete the activity in a day or two. Arrange to have the students receive a token, stamp, or treat of some kind as they visit each person and place in the school.

Welcome to________________________School.

This is a drawing of my school.

School Address:________________________

Phone Number:________________________

Fax Number: ________________________

Web Site/E-mail:________________________

My name:________________________

My grade:________________________

My teacher:________________________

My room number:________________________

I visited the office.

________________________ is the principal.

________________________ is the secretary.

They gave me this:

Some of the things I saw in the office are:

Black line masters on pages 105-106

I visited the library.

________________________ is the librarian.

Some of the things I saw in the library are:

I got this in the library:

I saw some of the classrooms.

Room Number	Grade	Teacher

________________________ gave me this:

Some of the things I really liked in the classrooms I saw are:

Black line masters on pages 107-108

Figure 1. Orientation activity

I found the washroom
closest to my classroom.
(draw what you saw)

I found the water fountain.
(draw what you saw)

I saw the gym.
(draw what you saw)

I saw the lunch area.
(draw what you saw)

I found the playground.
(draw what you saw)

The nurse is_____.

The counselor is_____.

All About Me

This is a drawing of me and my family.

My name in English is _____.

My name in another language is _____.

This is something I left behind when I came to this school.

Black line masters on pages 109-110

This was my old home, and this is
a drawing of my new home.

This is a drawing of my old school, and this is my
new school.

I am _____ years old, and my birthday is on _____.

I can _____.

I came to this school from _____.

I can speak _____, and I will learn English.

This is a drawing of some of the things I like:

Black line masters on pages 111-112

Figure 1. (cont'd) Orientation activity

CHAPTER 5

ASSESSMENT: FINDING OUT WHAT WE NEED TO KNOW

ARE TEACHERS GETTING THE RIGHT INFORMATION?

In many classrooms, teachers begin the new school year by learning the names of the students, establishing a timetable, and giving students a series of standardized assessments to determine their reading, writing, and math skills. Some teachers feel standardized tests are one of the best starting points for gathering information about students. Because the overriding need for the teachers is to obtain data quickly and easily, many do not examine the validity and reliability of the tests. Whether or not these tests are appropriate for the diverse learners in the class is never questioned. Standardized assessments, however, lack thought about who is being tested and how the grade levels and percentiles, calculated after scoring the test, are to be used to assist in planning and teaching a class of students.

We believe the time used to administer and write standardized tests is better spent gathering information about the students that is relevant to the skills required for success in the classroom. What teachers really want to know is how well their students can think, read and respond, problem solve, and express their ideas orally and in writing. This information goes well beyond the scope of most standardized tests.

WHAT WE DO FOR ASSESSMENT

As a team, we have designed some informal ways for gathering the kinds of information that help us get to know each student's strengths and needs (see figure 2). We are aware that, to be useful, the assessments should allow students to show their knowledge in a variety of ways. For example, traditional reading comprehension assessments that use a multiple-choice format do not give students a chance to explain their thinking or elaborate on their ideas. Scoring a multiple-choice reading subtest is fast and easy to do; however, the information is largely unusable when planning for teaching reading or writing skills.

Following a reading selection with open-ended questions is a much better way to determine how well each student reads, makes personal connections, and expresses his/her thinking in writing. A student's reflections provide rich information for getting to know him/her as an individual learner. Our assessment strategies must reflect our goals: to learn more about our students and to make carefully considered instructional decisions.

The assessment activities that follow were administered to grade-nine students. These assessments can be used with students at any grade level, with minor adaptations for grade appropriateness.

Reading Assessment

The reading assessment is designed to assess students' reading comprehension through written responses. Our students completed this assessment at the end of the first week of the school year.

In this assessment, students read a passage, and then answer three questions. The written passage is based on a topical newspaper article (any grade-appropriate text can be used). Since we are interested in gathering as much information about the students as we can, we ask the students to circle words that they are unfamiliar with as they read.

As the students read silently and respond, we listen to each student read aloud a portion of the passage. For those students who are absolutely unable to read the text, we read it, then the questions, to them. We modify the written task by asking them to use drawings. Sometimes it is helpful to have students who are fluent in both English and the first languages of the students clarify what we want shown. This process yields a great deal of pertinent information.*

The three questions that follow the passage are chosen to determine the students' understanding of what they have read at the literal, inferential, and evaluative levels. The first question asks students to construct a web that reflects their understanding of the ideas presented in the passage. The second question gives them the opportunity to write their explanation of an idiom used throughout the passage. The final question asks the students to write about their personal reactions based on their prior knowledge and a synthesis of what they have read. We encourage students who cannot respond in writing to respond with pictures. Whenever we cannot understand what the student has done, we follow up with a conversation about the passage and his/her response. We do not allow the format of the assessment interfere with what the student is demonstrating he/she knows and can do.

---

* Additional information on this form of assessment is found in chapter 4 of *Student Diversity: Addressing the Needs of All Learners in Inclusive Classrooms* by F. Brownlie and C. Feniak.

Wired to Buy

Have you heard of Generation Y, the Digital Generation, the Millennials, or the Echo Boomers? If you have not yet, you will very soon. Many executives in the corporate world of advertising are studying and surveying the habits and interests of the 78 million young people who have been born since 1978. By the year 2010, it is estimated that the population of teenagers will peak at 35 million! Such a large group of consumers has the corporate world trying to learn more about what teens want to buy.

Teens today are believed to have approximately 25 percent more income than teenagers did five years ago. It is well known that teens spend billions of dollars a year on clothes, and many of them use a credit card for those purchases. Advertisers are also aware that this generation of teens is the first computer-literate group of shoppers.

Today's teens are very used to seeing advertising, and they identify with specific brand names. Catalogs (in both print and computer formats) have been developed for teens to capitalize on their buying power. In addition to showing a selection of items that can be purchased, some of these catalogs include articles that highlight fashion news, health information, and advice about relationships. The on-line catalogs boast that they are open 24 hours a day for interested shoppers.

The producers of the Delia line of teen clothing and accessories have created an on-line catalog. Teens who visit Delia's web site have a chance to get free e-mail and the opportunity to build a home page. Discounts on Delia's products are offered for e-mail users who check their mail at this web site.

The advertising industry is betting on the success of on-line catalogs as a way to cash in on the revenue that the "wired generation" has. Keep an eye out for new advertising schemes that combine computer technology with sales. Even adults who are wary of making on-line purchases had better get ready to click their mouse!

the words that you do not already
questions. In your answers, try to
from your own experiences and from

ens in this article? Show this
and, if you wish, drawings.

y the term *wired generation.*

that you will use? Why or why not?

Black line masters on pages 113-114

Figure 2. Reading passage and questions to assess reading comprehension

SETTING CRITERIA FOR EVALUATION

When students are involved in setting the criteria for evaluation, they have a better understanding of the expectations and, therefore, become more aware of ways to improve their responses. The four-point performance scale (see figure 3) that we use was determined by the grade-nine students prior to their reading/writing assessment. Students become familiar with the terms – *powerful, competent, partial,* and *undeveloped* – as we use them throughout the year for tasks that include criteria-referenced assessment.

Our feedback to the students is directly related to the performance scale.. For example, Bobby, a student who was given a "partial" rating on the web question, can compare his response to both our comments and the performance scale and note that in the future his response should include more details (in this case, "statistics" and main points from the text).

While specifics of the performance scale change with the task being completed, the terminology, "powerful, competent, developing, undeveloped," remains the same.

4. Powerful
■ ideas are connected to evidence from the passage
■ personal experiences are included whenever relevant
■ demonstrates a very good understanding of the idiom used in the passage
■ insightful comments are included

3. Competent
■ several connections are made to evidence from the passage; answers include elaboration on ideas
■ some relevant experiences are included
■ good understanding of the idiom is demonstrated
■ comments are clear, specific, and complete

2. Partial
■ little evidence is presented to support ideas
■ personal experiences are included but they are not relevant
■ attempt is made to explain the idiom, but real understanding is not evident
■ comments are incomplete

1. Undeveloped
■ can identify some of the main ideas
■ quotes text instead of using his/her own words to rewrite ideas
■ no evidence of comprehension of the idiom
■ comments are incomplete

Figure 3. The four-point performance scale

WHAT WE KNOW AFTER THIS ASSESSMENT

After reading our students' responses (see figure 4), we can make some tentative judgments about their ability to read and respond. For example, students who are beginning to learn how to express their knowledge in English may be challenged by familiarity with the topic of the article, the reading level of the article, the vocabulary used, and/or their ability to express themselves fluently in English. With this information we can, therefore, begin to plan for instruction.

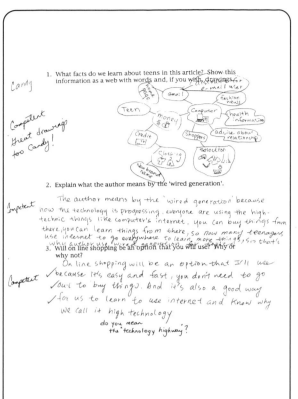

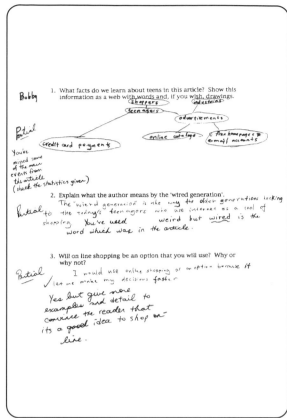

Figure 4. Two examples of students' responses, with evaluation notes

WHAT WE DO FOR AN ORAL LANGUAGE ASSESSMENT

Oral language assessment is another way we get to know our students, as well as a way to find out how well they communicate orally. First, we divide the class into pairs of students. Then we have the pairs of students interview each other and report the information to the rest of the class. This activity helps set the tone of the classroom as a place where speaking and listening skills are important and where collaboration with other students is integral to most activities. For ESL learners, it is particularly important to include questions pertaining to their past, present, and future. The questions also help us determine how well these students use language structures.

The activity is structured as follows:

1. Explain to students that they are each going to interview a classmate. Then, as a class, brainstorm the kinds of questions that might be interesting to ask during an interview.

2. Record the questions on the chalkboard so that the students can see each question and build on one another's ideas. If students do not mention it, suggest that they include questions about their partner's past and present activities, and their interests and goals for the upcoming school year.

3. Have students choose two questions from the student-generated list.

4. Have the students write down the questions they will ask during the interview.

5. Inform students they will be recording their partner's answers to questions during the interview.

6. Have students choose a partner who is not in their usual group of friends. This is a great way for everyone to get used to working with different classmates.

After the brainstorming session, suggest to students that they practice the interview with one of the adults in the room. Students are encouraged to ask the questions. The teacher who is not being interviewed helps build upon the questions asked in order to model how to draw more information from the person being interviewed.

Before the presentations, we give students ample class time to interview each other, organize the information, and practice the introduction of their partner. We also discuss the criteria for the oral presentations. Our grade-nine students identified the following points:

- voice needs to be heard
- can use notes but cannot read from them entirely
- information needs to be clear
- has to follow the directions given for the assignment

We often add several points that we feel are important components to be evaluated. We use a locally developed resource that was designed to help teachers observe, evaluate, and report on student performance (*British Columbia Evaluating Group Communication Skills Across Curriculum*, 1995)

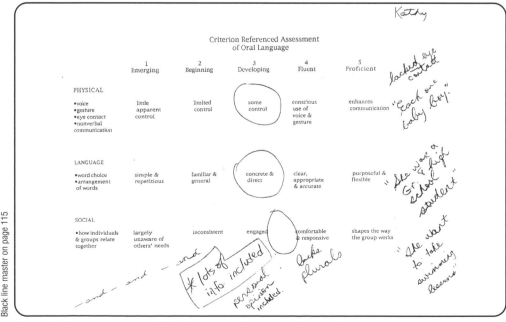

Figure 5. An assessment of Kathy's presentation, using Criteria Referenced Assessment of Oral Language Form

Black line master on page 115

as a model. Then we expand the student-generated criteria into a rubric and show the rubric on an overhead projector. Students then introduce their partners to the class.

Correct use of verb tense is not included on the criteria sheet. This omission is deliberate; ESL students often fixate on tense rather than on building their oral language competencies. Instead, we keep notes on student expertise in this area but do not use it as criteria. Our goal in this activity is communication.

We listen to each interview and use a highlighter pen to show where the students are in comparison to the rubric. Notes about each presentation are jotted down as we listen to the students. For the students learning English (or for those using non-standard English), we write down direct quotations of their language so that we have a record of the kinds of language structures that they use (see figure 5). This information gives us an indication of some of the skills to focus upon. Working together in the classroom, skills such as these can be taught to small groups of students as needed, rather than to the entire class.

IN THE PRESENT

Language Structures:

_____ goes to school at _____ .
_____ likes playing _____ .
_____ likes _____ .
_____ lives _____ .
_____ 's favorite _____ (color, movie, CD, TV show, singer) is
_____ .
_____ goes to _____ .
_____ is a _____ person.

Themes to build on include going to school, hobbies, living with others, favorite colors, friendship, worst nightmares, characteristics, television shows, movies, singers, reading books, family, and siblings.

IN THE PAST

Language Structures:

_____ was born in _____ .
_____ moved to _____ .
_____ visited _____ .
_____ traveled to _____ .
_____ went to school in _____ .
_____ used to live in_____ .

Themes to build on include birth place, previous schools attended, traveling, visiting, moving, and time.

IN THE FUTURE

Language Structures:

_____ wants to be _____ .
_____ would like to save for _____ .
_____ will be moving to _____ .
_____ will go back to _____ .
_____ will go to university to study _____ .
_____ would like to marry _____ .
_____ would like to be/have _____ .

Themes to build on include career interests (e.g., fashion designer, paleontologist, animator, dentist), hopes (e.g., get married, make friends, save money to buy…), marks, things to learn (e.g., how to meet girls, swim).

Figure 6. Language structures

Black line master on page 116

WHAT WE KNOW AFTER THIS ASSESSMENT

This assessment activity yields considerable information. We use many of the topics and ideas that come up during the interview to plan future lessons. Language structures that students know are also extended in future lessons (see figure 6).

HOW WE ORGANIZE AN ORAL READING ASSESSMENT

Students in elementary schools are involved in oral reading as a daily activity. As we listen to students read, we gather information about reading fluency, comprehension, understanding new vocabulary, and word attack skills. In secondary English classes, oral reading can provide the same kinds of useful information about student progress.

We are aware that oral reading assessments need to be completed quickly. In our grade-nine class, we needed to listen to thirty students in a short period of time. We decided that each student would be responsible for choosing a paragraph of text with no more than ten sentences from a grade-level

In our grade-nine class, five students were ESL learners. From the interviews, we found out the following information:

Places of origin:

- Korea, Taiwan, Hong Kong, China, Ukraine

Length of time in Canada:

- from two to five years. Most came directly from their country of origin; two came from their country to Canada via the United States.

Previous schooling:

- before entry into Canada, all had previous schooling at appropriate grade and age levels in their countries of origin. Two students attended school in the United States prior to entry into Canada.

Language background:

- all students were fluent in another language. All could read and write in their home languages. Several students were learning English as a third language. Some home languages were closer to English than others.

About the students as people:

- one student was moving; another saving for a computer. One of the boys wanted a girlfriend; another had no friends and wanted to make some. One student wanted to learn how to swim; another planned to return to Korea the following year to enter the army. Interests ranged from music, televisions, books, computers, and fashion to games.

Oral language:

- their ability to speak English with confidence and skill varied greatly. Some spoke quietly and slowly. Others were loud and confident. One student spoke with some interference from sounds in his home language.

All students were able to complete the interview. Their use of the English language varied greatly. For example, one student used mainly present tense verbs and nouns to describe immediate objects and familiar activities. Another used mainly future tense verbs and anticipated participation in a variety of activities for years to come. Some students struggled with past tense; for others it was easy. The choice of nouns varied from simple to more complex. Sentences also varied in length from short to longer and complex structures.

anthology of short stories and poetry. We gave the students class time to practice reading the passage fluently and to fill out a sheet (see figure 7) of five questions related to their reading.

1. Why did you choose this passage?

2. What were you thinking about when you read this passage?

3. How does this passage relate to your own experiences?

4. What do you want me to notice as I listen to you read?

5. What do you do when you are trying to read a word that you do not know?

For the next several class periods, students worked on individual tasks while we moved around listening to each student read. After the students finished reading, we asked several open-ended questions that pertained to what they had read. These included prediction-type questions such as, "What do you think might happen next in this story?" Vocabulary questions about specific words read in the text and questions relating to figures of speech contained in the passage were also asked. These questions provided a quick assessment of whether or not the student understood what he/she had read.

As each student read aloud, our observations were recorded on the second half of the assessment sheet. Short notes about word omissions and additions, pronunciation errors, and word attack skills were included. After students completed reading the passage, we shared our observations, giving them an indication of their understanding of the passage based on their answers to the questions. We make sure students view this experience as a useful activity that helps them learn more about how they are developing as readers. The purpose of assessment is to fuel learning, not to arrest it.

The last question asks students to describe the strategy they use when reading an unknown word. Their responses to this question provide immediate information for instruction planning. In our grade-nine class, many students indicated that they try to pronounce a word in the hope that they recognize it. Some students wrote that they read the passage and try to determine the meaning of the word by using context clues. With this information, we decided that, in addition to a class review of the use of context clues, some students would benefit from a series of small group "mini-lessons." These lessons can be conducted by the ESL teacher, the support teacher, or the classroom teacher.

When we designed these informal assessments, our goal was to gather information about our students quickly and efficiently so that we could make informed instructional decisions. These assessments provided us (the teaching team) with ample data for collaborative planning that met the needs of each learner in the class.

Figure 7. An assessment of Edison's reading, using the Oral Reading Assessment form

Black line master on page 117

CHAPTER 6

INDIVIDUAL ASSESSMENTS OF ESL STUDENTS NEW TO A SCHOOL

PROVIDING SUPPORT

ESL students arrive at schools throughout the year, not just at the beginning of the school year. Upon arrival, to ensure that they receive ESL support and services, they are often administered various standardized tests. Many of these tests are costly, require one-on-one administration and specialized training to administer, and are not normed for ESL learners. In addition, it is questionable whether or not the results of formalized assessments provide accurate information about students who, in a new school, often in an unfamiliar country, may experience culture shock for a considerable period of time.

We use an informal approach to facilitate making decisions about offering ESL support and services. Once initial, informal assessment is completed, schools can better monitor the needs of ESL students through curriculum-based assessments within the context of authentic classroom activities. These provide more concise information about the ESL learners' proficiency in English, about the skills and strategies that they use to support learning, and about sociocultural adjustment to the new school.

The individual assessment has three components: oral language (listening and speaking), written language, and reading comprehension. Each component considers both K-3 learners and ESL learners in grades 4 through 9. In addition, we use a tool we call Informal Descriptors of English Language Proficiency to quickly (and informally) highlight the results of the assessment under the categories: beginner, intermediate, or advanced language proficiency. These descriptors take into account both social and academic language proficiency.

ASSESSMENTS

Classroom teachers, in collaboration with ESL specialists or support teachers, can administer quick, informal assessments of proficiency that require learners to participate in various activities (see figures 8-14). Completed results can be kept in students' files for future reference and updated as needed.

ORAL ENGLISH LANGUAGE PROFICIENCY ASSESSMENT FOR KINDERGARTEN TO GRADE 3

Oral Interview and Activities

Name: _____

Date: _____

Initials of person who assessed the student: _____

Assessment Instructions:

- Ask the questions on the next page orally.
- Place a "check" where the student answers questions correctly.
- Write the student's *exact* response on the sheet.
- Place an *x* in spaces where the student is not capable of answering the question.
- Students with "advanced" English oral language skills will answer all of the questions correctly and relatively quickly. They may require support with the language of the classroom, which can be determined at a later date. "Intermediate" English language learners will answer more than one-third of the questions accurately. They may also require academic support and can be monitored over time in the classroom. "Beginners" will answer none or just a few of the questions. These students will require support immediately.

Scoring guide: responds accurately _____ (√)

response incomplete _____ (o)

no response _____ (x)

This is an initial assessment only to help organize support for beginners. All further assessments should be curriculum-based within the context of authentic classroom tasks.

ESL ORAL ASSESSMENT: GRADES K-3

Oral Interview and Activities

1. What is your favorite food? Why is it your favorite food?
2. What is your favorite game? Why is it your favorite game?
3. Tell me about your family.
4. How high can you count? (Prompt if there is no response, and see if the learner continues.)
5. Tell me the names of these shapes. (Show a triangle, square, rectangle, and circle.)
6. Tell me the names of these body parts. (Point to two or three body parts.)
7. Tell me the names of these colors. (Show red, white, black, blue, yellow, and orange.)
8. Tell me the letters of the alphabet. (Prompt if there is no response, and see if the learner continues.)
9. What country are you from?
10. Ask me what my name is.
11. Ask me where the library is.
12. Ask me where the washroom is.
13. Pass me the book please.
14. What do you like to play at home?
15. Draw a picture of your home. Tell me about your home. (Prompt with questions.)
16. Draw a picture of your family. Tell me about your family. (Prompt with questions.)
17. Tell me about this picture. Show the student a photo or picture with a familiar scene.

Observation Notes: Write brief comments about anything unusual that may need to be monitored. For example, observations may be recorded about the student's speech (impediments, fluency, volume) or about body language (gestures, tics, confidence).

Black line masters on pages 118-119

Figure 8. Oral English Language Proficiency Assessment forms, grades K-3

ORAL ENGLISH LANGUAGE PROFICIENCY ASSESSMENT FOR GRADES 4 TO 9

Oral Interview and Activities

Name: _____

Date: _____

Initials of person who assessed the student: _____

Assessment Instructions:

- Ask the questions on the next page orally.
- Place a "check" where the student answers questions correctly.
- Write the student's *exact* response on the sheet.
- Place an *x* in spaces where the student is not capable of answering the question.
- Students with "advanced" English oral language skills will answer all of the questions correctly and relatively quickly. They may require support with the language of the classroom, which can be determined at a later date. "Intermediate" English language learners will answer more than one-third of the questions accurately. They may also require academic support and can be monitored over time in the classroom. "Beginners" will answer none or just a few of the questions. These students will require support immediately.

Scoring guide: responds accurately _____ (√)

response incomplete _____ (o)

no response _____ (x)

This is an initial assessment only to help organize support for beginners. All further assessments should be curriculum-based within the context of authentic classroom tasks.

ESL ORAL ASSESSMENT: GRADES 4-9

Oral Interview and Activities

1. What are your first and last names?
2. How old are you?
3. When is your birthday?
4. Where do you live? What is your address/phone number?
5. What country did you come from? How long ago? Do you miss it?
6. Tell me three things about your last school. What did you study?
7. What did you do yesterday?
8. Tell me about some games or sports you like to play.
9. Ask me my name.
10. Ask me for a pencil.
11. Stand up, and touch your ear.
12. Sit down, and touch your nose.
13. Take the large red square, and put it under the small green triangle. (attributes)
14. Do you have a family (brother/sister/mother/father)? What are their names?
15. What is this called? (Point to various body parts.)
16. Describe the clothes that you are wearing.
17. Do you like to watch television? Tell me about something you have watched.
18. Draw a picture of your friend(s). What things do you like to do with your friends?
19. Tell me about this picture. (Show the student a photo or picture with a familiar scene.)

Observation Notes: Write brief comments about anything unusual that may need to be monitored. For example, observations may be recorded about the student's speech (impediments, fluency, volume) or about body language (gestures, tics, confidence).

Black line masters on pages 120-121

Figure 9. Oral English Language Proficiency Assessment forms, grades 4-9

WRITTEN ENGLISH LANGUAGE PROFICIENCY ASSESSMENT FOR KINDERGARTEN TO GRADE 3

Writing Activities

Name: _____

Date: _____

Initials of person who assessed the student:_____

Assessment Instructions

- Read the directions aloud to the student (see next page).
- "Beginners" will write very little and/or will take a long time to start writing. Their writing may involve a few letters of the alphabet or words spelled phonetically. They may copy letters or words and may not generate them on their own. They may also illustrate their ideas instead of write them.
- "Advanced" learners will write relatively quickly. They will be able to use their writing to show meaning in simple sentences. There will be evidence of connections between sentences and of few errors.
- "Intermediate" learners will write somewhere between the range of beginners and advanced learners. There will be words that are repeated, one or two simple sentences, some accurate and some phonetic spelling.
- Suggested topics are included on page 123. Both narrative and expository (academic) writing are possible.

Scoring guide: Beginning writer _____
Intermediate writer _____
Advanced writer _____

ESL WRITTEN ASSESSMENT, GRADES K-3

Directions:

Students will complete a writing sample to determine whether or not immediate ESL support and service is warranted. The writing will remain unedited and filed for future updating. This will establish a baseline for monitoring the development of writing over time.

Remember, this is just an initial assessment to give a baseline and to arrange immediate support for those students who need it. Beyond this, all writing assessments should be based on curriculum within the context of authentic classroom tasks.

1. Write four letters of the alphabet.

2. **Narrative Writing:** On a separate sheet of paper, write about a story you like.

3. **Academic Writing:** On a separate sheet of paper, write about an animal you like.

Black line masters on pages 122-123

Figure 10. Written English Language Proficiency Assessment forms, grades K-3

WRITTEN ENGLISH LANGUAGE PROFICIENCY ASSESSMENT FOR GRADES 4-9

Writing Activities

Name: _____

Date: _____

Initials of person who assessed the student: _____

Assessment Instructions

- Read the topic aloud to the student. Encourage the student to make notes, draw, talk, or make a web to plan ideas before beginning to write.
- "Beginners" will write very little and/or will take a long time to start writing. Their narrative writing may not have a noticeable sequence of events. Writing will consist of phrases with grammatical errors, short sentences, and simple ideas.
- "Advanced" learners will write relatively quickly, may plan first using a web or notes, and will write sentences of some complexity with few errors. Writing will have a logical sequence and order with a noticeable beginning, middle, and end.
- "Intermediate" learners will write somewhere between the range of beginners and advanced learners. There may be a combination of phrases and sentences, some errors, evidence of some sequence and transition words/phrases.
- Suggested topics are included on page 125; both narrative and academic writing are possible.

Scoring guide: Beginning writer _____
Intermediate writer _____
Advanced writer _____

ESL WRITTEN ASSESSMENT, GRADES 4-9

Directions:

Students will complete a writing sample to determine if ESL support and service is warranted. The writing will remain unedited and be filed for future updating. This will establish a baseline for monitoring the development of writing over time.

Remember, this is just an initial assessment meant to give a baseline and to arrange immediate support for those students who need it. Beyond this, all writing assessments should be based on curriculum within the context of authentic classroom tasks.

Narrative Writing

Topic: A Story I Know

Write about a story that you know because someone has told it to you, you have told the story to someone, or you read the story at some time in your life. Include as many details as you remember.

Academic Writing

Topic: What I Know About Science or Another School Subject That I Like

Write about a school subject that you like such as science, math, language arts, or social studies. Give as many descriptive details as you can about what you study in the subject. Explain why you like the subject.

Black line masters on pages 124-125

Figure 11. Written English Language Proficiency Assessment forms, grades 4-9

**ENGLISH LANGUAGE READING ASSESSMENT
FOR GRADES 4-9**

Reading Comprehension Activities

Name: _____

Date: _____

Initials of person who assessed the student:_____

Directions:

- Select a story at the appropriate age/grade level. Have the student read the story aloud to you. When the student is finished, ask him/her to retell the story to you. Record his/her responses under appropriate headings on the Retelling Response Record: Story form.

  You may wish to photocopy a page of the chosen text, and record the student's oral reading performance. The following codes can be used:

  - omission   ca̶t̶
  - repetition   <u>cat</u>
  - insertion   ⌃
  - self corrects   SC
  - don't know   DK
  - reversal   the|end
  - sounded out   SO

- Select a text of academic content at the appropriate age/grade level. Have the student read the text aloud to you. When the student is finished, ask him/her to retell the text and record his/her ideas on the Retelling Response Record: Information Text form.

- "Beginners" will be able to read isolated words, or they will read word by word. They will be able to repeat some words. Some beginners will only be able to describe the text from the drawings or pictures.

- "Intermediate" learners will retell some parts of the text. There will be evidence of decoding skills, and they will understand most of the meaning.

- "Advanced" learners will read relatively quickly and will retell most events and information accurately.

Note: Some teachers tape-record this informal assessment to make scoring easier.

Scoring guide: **Beginning reader**   _____

                   Intermediate reader   _____

                   Advanced reader   _____

Students who experience great difficulty reading basic material will require intensive support immediately.

Remember, this initial assessment provides a baseline and enables you to arrange immediate support for students who need it. Beyond this, all assessments should be based on curriculum within the context of authentic classroom tasks.

Figure 12. English Language Reading Assessment forms, grades 4-9

Name: _____ Grade: _____ Text: _____

Retelling Response Record: Story

Student's summary of the main idea or theme of the story.

Supporting ideas given by the student.

Student's description about the:

- Characters

- Setting

- Action

- Information that was/was not sequenced appropriately.

- Additional information volunteered when comprehension questions were asked (who, what, where, when, why, how).

Other comments about the retelling:

Figure 13. Retelling Response Record: Story form

Name: _____ Grade: _____ Text: _____

Retelling Response Record: Information Text

Student's summary of the main idea or theme of the story.

Supporting ideas given by the student.

Student's description about the:

- Main idea

- Relationship of the main idea to the meaning

- Details recalled

- Predictions made about meaning of the text

- Additional information volunteered when comprehension questions were asked (who, what, where, when, why, how). Relationship of student's own experiences to the information.

Other comments about the retelling:

Figure 14. Retelling Response Record: Information Text form

INFORMAL DESCRIPTORS OF ENGLISH PROFICIENCY IN READING, WRITING, AND ORAL LANGUAGE

The assessment sheets we use (see figures 15-17) barely skim the surface in terms of language proficiency. However, they provide a framework from which to build school-based descriptors in greater detail. They also facilitate the recording of information for ESL students who are new to the school.

The appropriate descriptors can be highlighted in yellow and dated, initialed, and filed as a baseline for following the progress of learners new to the school. Later in the year, the descriptors can be revisited and highlighted in another color, then dated, initialed, and filed.

The sheets can be completed by the classroom teacher, alone or in consultation and collaboration with the English language support teacher, and can be used

- as a starting point for planning lessons

- to develop criteria for marking student progress

- to help formulate an annual instructional plan for a student

- to report to parents or caregivers on a regular basis

- to report on student progress

- as a form of ongoing record keeping

- for providing a heading from which more specific details can be developed

- to monitor changes in student performance for school and district accountability

Note: ESL learners may be beginners for one, two, or more years; intermediate learners for three to seven years; and advanced learners for two or three more years depending upon their backgrounds and experiences. The descriptors are not meant to be tied to time but rather to language learning, both social and academic language.

INFORMAL DESCRIPTORS OF READING PROFICIENCY IN ENGLISH

FOCUS	BEGINNING/EMERGING	BEGINNING	INTERMEDIATE/DEVELOPING	INTERMEDIATE/EXPANDING	ADVANCED/PROFICIENT
Reading • narrative or literary	• virtually no proficiency in reading in English • listens to stories read aloud • can repeat some words • recognizes sound/symbol relationships • shows an awareness of print	• beginner reader English • can follow along with choral reading • can retell some parts of simple narrative texts • uses some phonics and/or other decoding skills	• reads basic, simple reading material in English • retells the beginning, middle, and end of most stories • recognizes plot, character, and the main story events • reads and understands some simple content/expository text	• expanding reading ability to include some content material in English • reads some narrative material independently • recognizes setting, character, plot, climax, conflict, and resolution in most stories • can read orally	• reads and understands general academic material in English • reads and understands general narrative and expository material • relates reading to experiences • uses a variety of reading strategies
• core academic content or expository	• shows an awareness that words have meaning	• reads simple descriptive lesson material	• makes regular use of the dictionary to seek word meanings	• has awareness of the meaning conveyed in poetry • can predict content and read between the lines sometimes and make inferences • comprehension of content vocabulary in core academic subject areas is expanding	• recognizes literary elements and genres • can extract important details from text • still reads below native-English speed and sometimes needs to use dictionary to aid comprehension • timed tests present some problems

Black line master on page 130

Figure 15. Informal Descriptors Assessment forms: Reading

INFORMAL DESCRIPTORS OF WRITING PROFICIENCY IN ENGLISH

FOCUS	BEGINNING/EMERGING	BEGINNING	INTERMEDIATE/DEVELOPING	INTERMEDIATE/EXPANDING	ADVANCED/PROFICIENT
Writing • narrative or literary • core academic content or expository	• virtually no proficiency in writing in English • writes letters or single, simple words • copies letters and simple words from a model • exhibits little awareness of spelling, capitalization, or punctuation	• beginner writer in English • writes or copies phrases and patterned, simple sentences • uses limited and repetitious vocabulary in writing samples • uses phonetic spelling • makes frequent errors in structure and spelling, obscuring meaning • writes very slowly	• writes basic, simple sentences in English • writes simple sentences in the present tense • has trouble with subject-verb agreement in writing • run-on sentences are common structures in writing and other errors • limited use of spelling, words, articles, prepositions, and word order • often omits endings and/or words • uses some capitalization, punctuation, and conventional spelling but continues to make some errors that interfere with comprehension	• expanding ability to write in literary and academic subject areas in English • able to write a simple paragraph with little elaboration of ideas • writing exhibits inconsistent use of a variety of verb tenses, subject-verb agreement, and other errors • limited understanding of paragraph organization • uses punctuation, capitalization, and transitional spelling • makes errors in sentence structure that do not interfere with meaning • has difficulty with written material under timed or test conditions • does not understand idioms • writes simple sentences about academic content but cannot collect information and write in detail • shows little ability to write expository/argumentative material/essays	• writes well both in literary/narrative and academic/expository • able to coherently connect more than one paragraph • able to elaborate on ideas • is able to present a main idea with supporting details • uses appropriate verb tenses most of the time • errors in sentence structure do not interfere with meaning • uses varied vocabulary that is appropriate for different styles/purposes • very few errors in mechanics — capitalization, punctuation, or spelling • writes with some errors in idioms • speed is improving but still writes below the speed of native-English writers

Black line master on page 131

Figure 16. Informal Descriptors Assessment forms: Writing

INFORMAL DESCRIPTORS OF ORAL LANGUAGE PROFICIENCY IN ENGLISH: SPEAKING AND LISTENING

FOCUS	BEGINNING/EMERGING	BEGINNING	INTERMEDIATE/DEVELOPING	INTERMEDIATE/EXPANDING	ADVANCED/PROFICIENT
1. Speaking	• virtually no English speaking proficiency	• begins to communicate personal and survival needs	• asks and answers questions about personal needs and familiar simple topics	• converses intelligibly in most social situations but academic conversations are challenging	• participates effectively in both social and academic conversations with only occasional idiomatic difficulties
(a) Fluency	• repeats an occasional word(s) • speech is halting and fragmented • limited or no social or classroom conversation • virtually no knowledge of English sentence structures	• frequent basic errors • uses one word utterances and short patterns or phrases in social conversation • usually hesitant and sometimes silenced by language limitations in the classroom	• speaks hesitantly, often rephrasing and searching for words and/or the correct manner of expression • speech is better in everyday conversations than in classroom discussions	• speaks with occasional hesitation • speech is generally fluent with occasional lapses while searching for appropriate expressions in classroom discussions	• speaks with near-native fluency — hesitations do not interfere with most communication • speech in both everyday conversations and classroom discussions is relatively effortless
(b) Structure	• virtually no English vocabulary	• many errors in grammar and order • must rephrase often	• uses mainly present tense verbs • omits words and endings often • frequent errors in applying rules of grammar and word order	• uses some sentence variety • inconsistency in applying rules of grammar • some errors in word order, endings	• grammatical usage and word order approximate that of a native-English speaker
(c) Vocabulary		• uses functional vocabulary • vocabulary is limited • frequent misuse of words	• uses limited vocabulary • conversation limited by lack of vocabulary in social and classroom discussions	• uses adequate vocabulary • few word usage errors • conversation in social situations is adequate • limited classroom conversation	• use of vocabulary and idioms approximates that of a native-English speaker in conversations, in social situations, and in the classroom • uses varied vocabulary

Figure 17. Informal Descriptors Assessment forms: Oral Language

INFORMAL DESCRIPTORS OF ORAL LANGUAGE PROFICIENCY IN ENGLISH (CONT'D)

FOCUS	BEGINNING/EMERGING	BEGINNING	INTERMEDIATE/DEVELOPING	INTERMEDIATE/EXPANDING	ADVANCED/PROFICIENT
2. Listening	• understands virtually no English conversation	• begins to understand words and phrases in conversations that help meet personal and survival needs	• understands and answers questions in conversation in most social situations but familiar experiences and topics are the main focus of comprehension	• understands conversation in most social and academic conversations but understanding presents difficulty	• understands both social and academic conversations with only occasional idiomatic difficulties
Aural Comprehension	• does not understand most English words and phrases	• understands a few social conversations when the topics are familiar • requires frequent repetition • has difficulty following conversations of any length • has difficulty following the sequence of simple directions • can only recall and retell a few events in a story	• can follow simple social conversations at English words and phrases but only if spoken slowly • understands most of what is said if it is spoken slowly • following classroom directions is difficult • does not understand conversations about most academic subject matter or content	• understands most social conversations at normal speed, both in and out of the classroom • understands most classroom discussions and uses requests for repetition, rephrasing, and clarification to support comprehension • has difficulty understanding conversations about academic subject content	• understands most social conversations at normal speed • can recall and retell most information heard in an appropriate sequence • understands most discussions of academic content in subject classes

Black line masters on pages 132-133

CHAPTER 7

BEGINNING LANGUAGE LEARNERS AND THEIR PARENTS

PREPARING BEGINNERS FOR SUCCESS IN THE CLASSROOM

ESL beginners need to be integrated into classrooms that are age and grade appropriate and with both specialist support and appropriate adaptations. Classroom teachers find it helpful if support teachers assist students in developing the following skills, which facilitate the successful integration of the students:

- some basic language of the classroom (of people, places, things, and events at school)

- knowledge about how to set up written assignments: in a notebook or on loose-leaf paper (name, date, title)

- basic understanding of the alphabet and basic reading skills

- printing and/or handwriting skills

- basic understanding of how to use the library; some research skills; an ability to take notes and use charts, maps, graphs, keys, and legends

- basic understanding of how to work with a textbook: table of contents, glossary, charts, graphs, and other components

- introduction to study skills, agenda books, work habits

- knowledge of the writing process and some editing skills

- knowledge of some simple learning strategies (e.g., KWL, webbing, key visuals)

- basic vocabulary

  - math/numeration system: core concepts and problem solving

  - social studies: core concepts

  - science: core concepts

  - basic language needed to participate in art, music, physical education (e.g., safety words, equipment)

- some cooperative learning experiences (e.g., working in pairs and/or in small and large groups)

- some exposure to problem-solving and open-ended activities

- understanding of basic classroom expectations and routines (e.g., turn taking, asking and answering questions, following basic directions)

- language needed to learn basic computer skills

- some metacognitive (reflecting on and learning about one's own learning) strategies (e.g., journals, reflective logs, reading logs)

All lessons developed for beginners need to focus on core concepts from the curriculum: all students, including beginners, need to use classroom curriculum themes as much as possible to develop their language and their thinking. Changes are made as appropriate to match student needs as they change over time. The goal is to fully integrate ESL learners into the classroom with appropriate support. Language learning is a time-consuming, ongoing process. It is not appropriate to separate ESL learners from their peers for extensive periods of time, and then to expect them to fit in socially and culturally.

HELPING BEGINNERS COPE IN THE CLASSROOM

Teachers can support all beginning ESL learners of any age by

- making them feel safe and secure.

- including examples of their cultures and languages in the artifacts in the classroom.

- giving them the right to speak in their first languages while learning English.

- making errors a normal and natural part of learning.

- accepting and rewarding all attempts at using the English language.

- giving students the right to be silent for a period of time while taking in the new language and culture that surround them.

- giving ESL students more "think" time and "write" time. Learning oral and written English for both social and academic purposes is hard and takes time.

SUPPORTING ESL LEARNERS IN GRADES K-3

Ten things you can collect to support the learning of K-3 ESL beginners who arrive in your classroom are:

1. picture cards with a thematic focus and word cards to represent them. Move from picture collections of topics closest to the learner (such as feelings, clothing, or body parts) to those more distant in time and space (such as things found in the classroom, around the school, at home, or in the community).

2. pictures that develop knowledge of concepts related to the curriculum. Concepts may include weather, seasons, trees, shapes, buildings, people, signs, ways of traveling, musical instruments, or color.

3. word banks: Build a bank of key words supported with illustrations or pictures related to your themes.

4. audiotapes of simple, repetitive, predictable books. Have a classroom volunteer read and tape-record a collection. Place each tape and the accompanying book in a plastic bag, and set up a listening center or tape recorder with headphones. Once students have learned the language of a pattern book or rhyme, they can make their own booklets, then take their booklet home and read with parents. For example, change the language of the rhyme, "Row, row, row your boat" to "Stow, stow, stow your coat."

5. stories, sequence cards, or action strips that students can order or reorder and talk about.

6. wordless books, bilingual books, and books with multicultural images.

7. alphabet and/or word cards and tracers.

8. scrapbook collage with pictures and words that represent survival vocabulary in English (such as how to ask for help, locate the washroom or nurse's room, or name feelings).

9. small booklets for photocopying where students draw a picture and add words to a simple sentence frame underneath.

10. direction cards, photos, or charts that clearly illustrate the daily routines and demonstrate directions.

SUPPORTING ESL LEARNERS IN GRADES 4-9

Ten things you can do to support the learning of ESL beginners in grades 4 to 9 who arrive in your classroom are:

1. Encourage students to write/illustrate journals daily. Students can write and draw at first and use both their first language and English until they are comfortable enough to make the shift.

2. Establish clear routines, and give directions one step at a time. Illustrate or photograph the routines/directions that are difficult to grasp quickly or that involve the students' safety in the gym or in a lab situation.

3. Demonstrate how to complete tasks. Give beginners examples or models of correct forms of the task or activity so that the expectations are clear.

4. Build a collection of wordless books for mature students and collections of bilingual books and books with multicultural images that have age- and grade-appropriate themes. Create simple tasks that involve illustrating the ideas in these books. Students can respond to these ideas by writing in English or another language and by drawing.

5. Build a collection of subject content task cards that have age- and grade-appropriate content and visuals or illustrations to complete that go with

them. Students can write in their first language, draw, or complete framed sentences or graphic organizers in English in response to the content.

6. Have the English-speaking students in the class create a scrapbook that illustrates survival vocabulary in English (such as how to ask for help, locate the washroom or nurse's room, or name feelings). Have them add ideas that they think are important for the new ESL students to know.

7. Build a classroom collection of leveled readers or reading material, both narrative and expository. Ensure that the content of the leveled readers is age, grade, gender, and culturally appropriate.

8. Create a collection of hands-on experiences that teach strategies that support learning and thinking: classifying words, ideas, and objects; sorting words, ideas, and concepts; ordering and reordering sentences or action strips; comparing and contrasting people, places, or things. Put each strategy in a labeled envelope or file folder. Vary the content so that there are a classifying activity that involves grouping living and nonliving things in science and a compare-and-contrast activity that involves two characters from a play, book, or movie in language arts.

9. Collect novels at a variety of reading levels with themes that are age, grade, gender, and culturally appropriate. Have a volunteer read and record some of the beginning novels so that students can hear the words read in English and get a feel for the flow of the language.

10. Build word banks of key words or survival words that are important to know in each subject area. These could be science words about energy, social studies words that explain culture or community, art words for describing paintings or sculptures, core vocabulary in music and physical education, and words for good citizenship. Be sure to include first-language translations, illustrations, and pictures or photos whenever possible.

WORKING WITH PARENTS WHO ARE NEW TO THE SCHOOL

Parents from culturally and linguistically diverse backgrounds also need consideration at school if they are to be meaningful participants in learning. Teachers can show respect for parents or caregivers by using translators at conferences whenever possible. In addition, establish a long-term plan for enhancing communication that is effective so that parents of ESL learners become involved wherever possible. Language should not be a barrier to participation.

In one successful program, the existing parent body, the Parent Advisory Committee, ensures that non-English as well as English-speaking parents have access to their meetings. This is done by having notices of meetings translated, suggesting that parents bring translators to meetings with them, and/or inviting translators along to meetings. In addition, parents have created a buddy-parent system: New parents are paired with a family that speaks the same language and that can provide support by answering questions about school and its activities.

In another successful program, the Parent Advisory Committee sets up meetings at a convenient time to introduce parents to those who provide services to schools: the counselor, the nurse, the speech language pathologist, the school psychologist, community liaison staff, multicultural workers, administrators, and teachers who provide resource support. At the meetings these individuals introduce themselves and briefly explain how they help students and families at school. Translators are available, and they translate the explanations for parents. Parents then ask questions in their first languages and these questions and answers are translated. At the end of the meeting, the group spends time socializing. These meetings offer opportunities for parents of ESL students to become aware of services offered at school. The meetings also give new parents a chance to ask questions and learn about how things work in the new school. As parents become familiar with those who support the education of their children, their comfort level increases.

COMMUNICATING WITH PARENTS THROUGH VIDEO REPORT CARDS

Communicating classroom events to parents of new ESL students can be challenging. Often a school's viewpoint needs to be communicated in a way other than by a traditional report card. A videotape is a successful method. Most families, even those living in the inner city, have access to a VCR.

Teachers Ann Vicente of Vancouver and Mike Smale of Los Angeles use videotapes to communicate to the parents of their students. Ann and Mike report far-reaching benefits when parents are given a videotape of their child's progress at the end of the school term. Parents learn how schooling may differ in Canada and in the United States from their native country. They see their children learning in a variety of situations, and they see how teachers encourage students to communicate in pairs, small groups, and classroom discussions. These videotapes often become treasured family keepsakes that are watched again and again — an indication that parents are very interested in learning more about their child's school experiences.

Each student needs a labeled, sixty-minute videotape. The tape and the video camera need to be accessible to the students at all times. Only a basic knowledge of operating the camera is required to make this method of communication successful!

Some activities that can be captured on videotape include:

- oral reading
- math and science activities
- art projects
- oral presentations
- special events

- class discussions

- the writing process

- small-group work emphasizing collaborative skills

- physical education activities

- student explanations/reflections in both English and their first language

- a student's choice of activities for his/her parents to see

- spontaneous moments: "That's a great_____. Let's videotape it."

It is possible to train older students to videotape students who want to include a specific activity on their video. No editing is done to these videos, so the teacher's voice is often heard.

At the end of the term, review a student's videotape prior to writing the report card (you will find the videotape contains much useful information). Watching the video can provide more information than a set of notes since the context of the learning is present. In addition, progress in oral-language development over a term is demonstrated, and goals for further growth are evident.

When parents and their child watch the videotape together, the tape may help to do the following:

- Stimulate conversation in their first language about the activities they are watching.

- Enhance parent-student conversation about school. The video helps to clarify what is done at school. Parents find some answers to the eternal question, "What did you do at school today?"

- Allow parents to better understand some of the points made through the translator during parent-teacher conferences. The translator can also view parts of the video if the parents want clarification of an activity they have seen.

- Help to foster more positive home-school relations. Parents tend to send the videotape back at the beginning of the new term so that the taping can continue.

COMMUNICATING WITH PARENTS: USING A STUDENT-LED CONFERENCE FORMAT

Student-led conferences support the learning of ESL students: the conferences offer students opportunities to show their successes to their parents and to be more active, knowledgeable participants in the assessment process. The student and the parent meet in a positive situation and share ideas – in any language – about learning.

This conference format replaces the traditional parent-teacher format. Several conferences are scheduled simultaneously in different areas of the room. Students, including ESL learners, explain their schoolwork to their parents. Students demonstrate their learning in various ways; for example, with portfolios and/or with short presentations at different learning centers. Typically, students and their parents spend half an hour discussing the student's progress, giving the teacher enough time to move from group to group to converse with each family.

To have parent-student conferences run smoothly, do the following:

- Have students keep a portfolio of their term's work, highlighting their academic progress and their progress learning English. Writing samples are particularly useful.
- With the guidance of the teachers, have students complete the Student-Led Conference form (see figure 18 or 19).
- Before the conference, have students practice explaining the contents of their portfolio to one another. Students, especially primary students, may follow a map or an itinerary of what to talk about and what to show.
- At the conference, have the student share the portfolio and follow his/her itinerary with his/her parents.
- Encourage parents to write on the Parents' Comments form in either English and/or in the language used at home (see figure 20). They can complete the form during the conference, after viewing the schoolwork and listening to their child's explanations. If the parents seem uncomfortable with writing, teachers can interview them about their impressions of their child's learning.

STUDENT-LED CONFERENCE FORM: GRADES K-3

Name: ____________________ Date: ______________

A drawing and/or words that show the work that I am proud of:

A drawing and/or words that show something I am trying to change:

A drawing and/or words that show my goals:

For Friends	For School Work	For Myself

Black line master on page 134

Figure 18. Student-Led Conference form Grades K-3

STUDENT-LED CONFERENCE FORM: GRADES 4-9

Name: ______________________________ Date: ______________

Work that I am proud of:

Some things I know I need to work on:

Three goals for next term

Social: ______________________________

Academic: ______________________________

Personal: ______________________________

Black line master on page 135

Figure 19. Student-Led Conference form Grades 4-9

- If translators are available, use them during or after the conference. However, one of the main goals of the conference is the active participation of the parent.

PARENTS' COMMENTS

What I am proud of:

____
____
____
____
____
____

How I will support your learning:

____
____
____
____
____
____

Student's signature: ______________________________

Parent's signature: ______________________________

Black line master on page 136

Figure 20. Parents' Comments form

PARENTS AS COLLABORATORS: ENCOURAGING PARENT INVOLVEMENT IN LEARNING

Something as simple as listening to a child read in any language on a regular basis supports academic development. Parents can do many other things to support learning at school even if they are not fluent speakers of English. The black line masters (see figures 21 and 22) can be translated into the languages of your school and included in report cards or distributed at conferences. The forms provide specific suggestions for ways that parents of ESL students can support learning.

> The researchers found that children who read to their parents made significantly greater progress in reading than those who were given additional reading instruction, and this was particularly true for children who, at the beginning of the project, were experiencing difficulty learning to read.
>
> —J. Cummins in L. Spangenberg-Urbschat and R. Pritchard (eds.); *Kids Come in All Language*

TEN THINGS PARENTS CAN DO AT HOME TO SUPPORT THE LEARNING OF ESL STUDENTS, GRADES K-3

1. Visit the local library on a regular basis. Ensure your child has a library card and is able to use it. Accompany your child for story times at the library.

2. Set aside at least fifteen minutes a day for family reading. Read to your child in English and/or in the language of the home, and listen to your child read. Read both stories and information books about people, places, things, and events. Talk about who is in the pictures, where they are, what is happening, why it is happening, and make predictions about what will happen next.

3. Visit places in the community with your child to encourage new interests. These places can be the beach, the woods, a science center, museums, art galleries, and anything else your community has to offer.

4. Take an interest in writing by having your child draw and talk to you about what he/she has created. Write a description of the drawing for your child in English and/or in the language of the home.

5. Together, explore the print in magazine and newspapers, on signs, and in the community at large.

6. Create a place within the home that is quiet and free from distractions where your child can do school work.

7. Keep a scrapbook of your child's work so he/she knows that you value what is being done. Provide your child with positive feedback about his/her progress in learning.

8. Support your child's developing bilingualism. He/she is not replacing the language of the home with English. Your child is becoming bilingual. Studies show that those with command of both English and the language of the home are, in the long term, more likely to have success as a learner.

9. Attend parent-teacher conferences, and ask for a translator if you need one.

10. Become involved in your child's school, if possible, by helping out with school activities such as field trips and other school events.

Black line master on page 137

Figure 21. Ten things parents can do to support K-3 ESL learners

TEN THINGS PARENTS CAN DO AT HOME TO SUPPORT THE LEARNING OF ESL STUDENTS, GRADES 4-9

1. With your child, visit the local library on a regular basis. Ensure your child has a library card and is able to use it.

2. Set aside at least twenty minutes a day for family reading. Encourage your child to read novels (in any language) and a variety of information books about people, places, things, and events from the past, present, and future. Read books with geographical maps, drawings and sketches, diagrams, charts, graphs, or photographs.

3. Together, visit places in the community to encourage your child to develop new interests. Some suggestions are the beach, the woods, a science center, museums, and art galleries. Ask your child to tell you what he/she is learning at school.

4. Take an interest in writing by having your child write in a private diary or journal, or by writing to friends and family at home. Encourage your child to experiment with different forms of writing: poems, information, stories, lists, flow charts, letters of persuasion.

5. Create a place within the home that is quiet and free from distractions where your child can do school work

6. Help your son/daughter to get organized. Set up a daily schedule with a routine work/study time, and monitor homework. Offer positive support and suggestions as needed.

7. Help your child learn strategies for managing the information in textbooks and for note-taking. Find books in the library on study skills, enrol your child in a mini-course, or ask teachers or the teacher-librarian at your child's school for ideas.

8. If you can afford to hire a tutor, ask the tutor to help your child develop note-taking skills, strategies for learning, and study skills. In addition to working on classroom assignments, some of the time with the tutor should be used to "learn how to learn."

9. Monitor the amount of time your son/daughter spends on games on the computer, on chat-lines, and on e-mail.

10. Be positive and supportive. Balance time for study with time for play. Learning should be something that brings pleasure, not a chore that takes away from free time: ensure your child has time for activities other than the formal learning of English. Keep in mind that much language acquisition occurs in social situations.

Black line master on page 138

Figure 22. Ten things parents can do to support 4-9 ESL learners

CHAPTER 8

LESSON PLANS AND UNIT PLANS

We designed the lessons and units that follow to be used in several contexts:

- in the regular classroom with the classroom teacher

- in a pull-out or separate class location with the English-language support teacher

- in the regular classroom when the classroom teacher and the English-language support teacher are working together in the classroom

In designing these lessons, we have modeled a variety of classroom organizations:

- a whole-group plan with whole-group direct instruction

- small group practice, encouraging the social nature of language learning

- individual response and accountability

We have also addressed multiple intelligences. In the lesson plans, the coding for these intelligences is as follows:

- **VL:** verbal linguistic – learning related to words and language, spoken and written

- **LM:** logical mathematical – learning related to scientific thinking, deductive thinking, numbers, and abstract patterns

- **VS:** visual spatial   learning related to visualizing and creating mental images

- **BK:** bodily kinesthetic – learning related to physical movement

- **MR:** musical rhythmic – learning related to tonal patterns, environmental sounds, and rhythm and beat

- **Interp:** interpersonal – learning related to relationships and communication

- **Intrap:** intrapersonal – learning related to reflection, metacognition, and inner states of being

- **N:** naturalist – learning related to patterns in nature

LESSON PLANS

MAKING THE WRITING PROCESS WORK WITH ESL LEARNERS

Resources

photographs or pictures

chart paper

felt pens

Purpose

After observing a series of photographs or pictures students are expected to begin to develop their skills at writing and editing. Some ESL students may just be learning to write; however, they will learn quickly when they participate in writing and editing with peers and with a teacher who supports and models the writing process.

The strategy involves teaching students how to manage their writing by explicitly instructing them on how to develop and improve writing. With a new tool to help them manage their writing, students will begin to write more freely and with greater success because they are building on skills acquired over time.

Student Participation

VS

Interp

VL

The Process

Grades 1-3

1. As a class, read a picture book.

2. Reread the book, and have the students choose one page they want to make into a class book.

3. Using the students' ideas, write a sentence frame on chart paper (e.g., Clouds are _____.) Have the students copy the sentence frame and complete it. You may wish to have them practice on individual chalkboards before writing the sentence in their journals.

4. Give each student a sheet of paper to print a sentence on and, if appropriate, to illustrate. ESL beginners can illustrate the idea, and the teacher can scribe the sentence for them.

5. Have each student read his/her completed sentence at a class meeting.

6. Collect all the pages and compile them in a class book, either a small book or a big book. Read the book as a class, and start a collection of

students' writing (each time, increase the complexity of the sentence and/or the words).

7. Give all ESL beginners a copy of the class book as part of the home reading program.

Grades 4-9

1. Set up a display of photographs or pictures that evoke an emotion (e.g., happiness, sadness) or highlight an image (e.g., orcas swimming, snow, tall buildings). Choose age- and grade-appropriate photographs or pictures.

2. Have the students observe the display and record their ideas about how they feel or what they see.

3. Have each student write the first sentence of a paragraph about one of the photographs or pictures (e.g., Happiness feels...; Tall buildings remind me of...; Walking in snow was...; Orcas swimming make me feel...).

4. As a class, read the sentences and build on the ideas. Spelling and grammar are not edited at this point: the focus is on the ideas.

5. Have each student choose one sentence and write four additional sentences about the topic, using details from the display.

6. Circulate, and support writing with words and ideas.

7. Organize the students into groups of four, and have them silently read one another's writing. When all members of the group have read the writing, they can discuss the strengths of the writing and ways that the writing could be built upon and/or improved.

8. Have students rewrite their first draft of the paragraph, improving the ideas and building details. When it is completed, conference with each student to discuss editing the structure: spelling, grammar, and format.

9. Have each student rewrite the first paragraph with appropriate editing.

10. When all students have completed their paragraph, discuss the next two paragraphs they are going to write. Again, as a class, create a topic sentence for each paragraph using ideas from the display. Follow steps 3-9.

11. As a class, brainstorm ideas about the type of language that helps bring closure (e.g., to conclude, in the end, in the future, in summary).

12. Have each student write a closing paragraph.

13. When students have completed their writing, have them silently read one another's work in small groups.

14. Have students illustrate the paragraphs.

15. Collect the writings, and publish a class book for future reading. If there are a large number of ESL learners, give each student his/her own copy to practice reading English at home and in the classroom.

A WALL OF SENTENCES: TEACHING SENTENCE STRUCTURE IN A MEANINGFUL WAY, GRADES 1-9

Resources

classroom curriculum

sentence strips

individual chalkboards

felt pens

Student Participation

VL

Interp

VS

Purpose

Students are more motivated to write when they draw from their own background experiences rather than from those of someone else. Sentence structure is taught using sentences that students have generated.

As a class, decide on a topic to write about. Each student then contributes one sentence, and a "wall of sentences" is built. The "wall of sentences" is used to build grammar skills and to support reading and writing.

The Process

1. Each day, choose a topic or theme.

2. Have students compose a sentence.

3. Have ESL beginners each dictate one sentence, which is scribed onto an individual chalkboard by the teacher. Each student then copies the words onto a sentence strip, adding illustrations as appropriate.

4. Have advanced learners write their own sentence on a sentence strip, using colored felt pens.

5. Place all sentence strips one above the other on a wall in the classroom, creating a wall of sentence strips.

6. Each day, read aloud all of the sentence strips chorally as class begins.

    - **Monday:** The focus is on nouns, which students list, count, and illustrate.

    - **Tuesday:** The focus is on verbs. Students try to find as many as they can, then illustrate or perform the action.

- **Wednesday:** The students examine the sentence frames, count how many different kinds there are, and think of new ones that are similar.

- **Thursday:** The focus is on adverbs and/or adjectives. Students list these and think of new ways of using them. The sentences are changed from statements to questions or exclamations.

- **Friday:** Students cut up some or all of the sentences and re-arrange the words to form new sentences.

7. Have students choose some of the sentences to record for reading at home, or the teacher can provide a sheet listing the sentences for continued reading at home.

Sample, Grades K-3

Topic: Trees

The students have looked at pictures of trees, and they have generated the following sentences.

A tree has leaves.
The branch is broken on my tree.
Trees grow from seeds.
Birds live in my tree.

The nouns generated include *tree, yard, leaves,* and *seeds.*
The verbs generated include *is, grow,* and *live.*
As a class, adverbs and adjectives are identified.

The sentences are changed from statements to questions and/or exclamations:

Is the tree green?
Is there a swing in your tree?
There's a bird in my tree!

Students take home a sheet listing all of the sentences.

Sample, Grades 4-9

Topic: Forts

A fort is a walled city.
A fort has a blacksmith shop.
Forts have a general store.
People used to live in forts for safety.

DEVELOPING VOCABULARY, GRADES 1-9

Resources

curriculum concepts

colorful pictures or photos

graphic organizer on an overhead

chart paper

Student Participation

VS

Interp

VL

Purpose

In many classrooms, teachers struggle with how to teach vocabulary to ESL learners without having them memorize long lists of words. Memorizing may be a way of learning that is familiar to some ESL students; however, many former ESL students can recall receiving long lists of English words that had form (they could spell and write the words) but no context or meaning (they did not know how to use the words appropriately). This lesson provides a way of teaching new vocabulary in context to beginners, intermediate learners, and more advanced learners of English.

With this strategy, beginners, intermediate, and more advanced learners of English use pictures, objects, field trips, experiments, experiences in class, and/or videos to build their vocabulary. When students learn words within the context of activities that interest them, their vocabulary grows because it has meaning for them.

Examine core concepts in curricula, and choose ideas from which to build vocabulary. ESL learners need to learn the vocabulary of the curriculum. Plan open-ended activities that will support ESL learners and extend the language of native-English-speaking students as well.

The Process

1. Collect large calendar-sized pictures of the concept (e.g., fish), and display them on the wall.

2. Ask students for words that describe the concept.

3. Organize the words generated by the students by topic on a web on chart paper or an overhead.

4. Model how to write a descriptive passage.

5. Have the students write their own paragraphs and illustrate them. (Some students may want to create their own webs and write on a new topic.)

Sample, Grades K-9

Topic: Fish

The teacher displayed ten large calendar-sized pictures of fish. She then created a web on the overhead with the word *fish* in the center. The students looked at the pictures and generated several words that described fish. The teacher added the words to the web, helping the students organize the words into categories when appropriate.

The teacher modeled the writing of a paragraph by asking the students to help her write a descriptive passage using words from the web. This is the paragraph she wrote:

Describing Fish

There are many different kinds of fish. All fish have tails, fins, and eyes. Fish can be large or small. Some fish are brightly colored, others are dull and uninteresting. Fish are found in lakes, rivers, or in the ocean. We fish for food and for pleasure.

Next, in small working groups of three, the students created their own webs and generated their own writing. They then shared their paragraph with another group. (Younger learners will write less, while older learners tend to write more.)

Beginners used the following pattern:

Description of Fish

There are many different kinds of fish. All fish have _____, _____, and _____. Some fish are _____, others are _____. Fish are found in _____. We fish for _____.

Teachers can also hand out the sentence frames on a sheet of paper and have all students fill in the blanks. Intermediate and advanced learners will build on the pattern.

A follow-up lesson might include having students label a diagram of a fish.

VISUAL SORT AND PREDICT, GRADES 1-9

Resources

Black line masters (illustrations by Janice Keyes) (see pages 139-142)

The Bear by John Schoenherr

Beyond the Ridge by Paul Goble

The Black Falcon retold by William Wise

The Great White Man-Eating Shark by Margaret Mahy

Student Participation

VL

VS

BK

Interp

Purpose

Schema theory suggests that enhancing a reader's background before reading increases his/her comprehension of text. However, making predictions about a story based on a series of words can be a challenging activity for students with a limited understanding of English.

In this exercise, students make predictions from illustrations and are supported in the reading process. The use of illustrations instead of words provides students with a visual context for organizing their thinking. Participating in small-group discussions about the illustrations of a story helps to activate prior knowledge and increases their comprehension of the story.

The Process

1. Divide the class into heterogeneous groups of three or four students.

2. Give each group a page from the black line master showing 6-8 illustrations or scenes from a story (see figure 23). With older students who are using texts without illustrations, scenes from the story can be interpreted in a series of teacher-made drawings.

3. Have the students cut out the drawings and discuss each illustration as to what is happening and where it fits sequentially in the story.

4. Have each group present its predictions (in the form of a story) to the rest of the class.

5. Have the students read the story individually or with a buddy, or read the story aloud to the class.

6. Students can then compare their predictions to the actual story: Have them write two paragraphs comparing and contrasting their predictions with the events in the story. (Younger students can retell the text's version orally).

Figure 23. Scenes from four stories

VISUAL SORT AND PREDICT WITH STUDENT DRAWINGS, GRADES 2-9

Resources

Chin Chiang and the Dragon's Dance by Ian Wallace

Chart paper or overhead

Student Participation

VS

Intrap

Interp

Purpose

Building relevant background knowledge prior to reading supports students' comprehension. Using this background knowledge, students interpret scenes from a story through a series of drawings. They can then use these drawings for a Visual Sort and Predict in the story.

In this lesson, students are given a series of statements from a story. They draw their own interpretations of the statements, then compare their drawings with each other. In this way, they work with images and language samples from the text before they read the story. The brain works with these samples to make connections in its natural search for patterns.

The Process

1. Choose a series of scenes from a story, and write out sentence-long descriptions on chart paper or the overhead. Do not have the scenes follow the story sequence. For example:

    The boy is proudly leaping and dancing at the tail of a dragon for the Chinese New Year Parade (see upper right box of work sample, figure 24).

2. Read each statement aloud, and have the students draw what they imagine each scene looks like.

3. After the students have illustrated each statement, give them an opportunity to look at and discuss one another's interpretations of the scenes.

4. As a class, select a drawing to represent each scene. Construct a master sheet for a Visual Sort and Predict.

5. Read the story so that students can compare the class master to the actual story.

Figure 24. One student's interpretation of scenes from a story

QUICK DRAW, GRADES 2-9

Resources

black line master (reproduced on 11 x 17-inch paper) (see page 143)

Student Participation

VL

VS

BK

Interp

Purpose

Students often have difficulty coming up with ideas for writing interesting narrative compositions. Quick Draw is a motivating way for students to work together in small groups and create a series of drawings that provide a visual story map.

Visual story maps greatly assist students who are learning to write. Visual plans provide structure for developing a story with a simple plot and relevant vocabulary through small-group discussions. For younger students, structure is important in developing good narrative writing. Older students can use Quick Draw as a prewriting activity to learn how to incorporate more detail into their writing.

The Process

1. Divide the class into heterogeneous groups of three or four students.

2. Give each group a copy of the black line master (see figure 25).

3. Give one student in each group twenty seconds to draw something related to the category in first space on the sheet. One after another, give each student in the group twenty seconds to add to the drawing. Have the students who are not drawing watch the progress of the member who is illustrating to plan what they will add (so that their ideas connect with and expand the initial drawing).

4. Follow step 3 for each category on the black line master.

5. Have students discuss the drawings in their groups and add related phrases and words around the illustrations.

6. Invite students to participate in a Gallery Walk: walk around the classroom and view the work produced by the other groups.

7. Have each student write a narrative based on anything he/she has seen or thought of during this exercise (see figure 26), including all of the parts of the story map.

Figure 25. A group of students in grade 2 created this Quick Draw

Andy   The Snowman
Once upoum a time there
was a Snowman he was a
Big fat Snowman and one day
a boy was up in a
tree and the sonwman help
the boy come back Down.
the boy Sad thankyou
to the sonwman the
sonwman sad do you want
to come was me the boy
sad ok! They went to a
tree huose the boy sad
whnt the haose was so
many souw.

Figure 26. Andy, an ESL student in grade 2, has been at the school for a year and a half

FREE VERSE POETRY, GRADES 3-9

Resources

Sadako by Eleanor Coerr

overhead projector and sheets

black line master (see page 144)

Student Participation

VL

VS

MR

Interp

Purpose

Writing poetry is often considered to be a challenging task for students, especially for those who are learning English. However, we find free verse poetry to be enabling for all students, allowing them to gain control over expressive language.

Asking students to record their thinking as they listen to a powerful story gives each student a means to remember striking aspects of the text.

The Process

1. Choose a compelling story with illustrations such as *Sadako* to read aloud to the students.

2. Divide the class into small heterogeneous groups.

3. Select four illustrations from the text. Ask the groups to respond to each picture by recording all of the thoughtful questions that the group members have (see figure 27). Circulate throughout the class and show an illustration and ask the groups to respond to the question, "What are you wondering?" Students can take turns scribing the questions that are contributed by others in the group.

4. After the students have all contributed their questions, show the next illustration and repeat this process with each of the four illustrations. Each student is then given a copy of the black line master.

5. Read the story aloud, and have students record their thinking in each of the four squares as they listen to the story. Show the illustrations that accompany the text as the story is being read aloud.

6. Record the students' favorite words and phrases (from their black line masters) on the overhead.

7. Have the students choose the words and phrases that they wish to include in a poem describing the text. Students can then experiment with order, flow, and rhythm of the language to form a free verse poem (see figure 28).

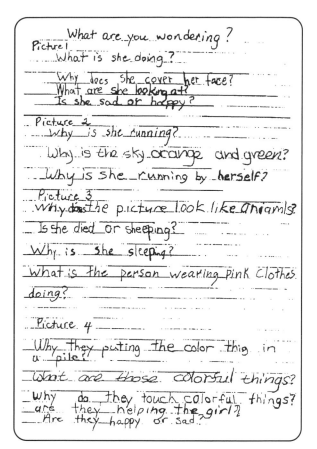

Figure 27. One group of students responded to the illustrations by asking these questions

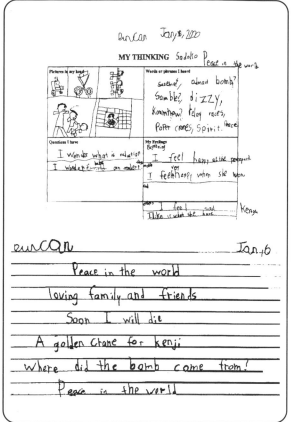

Figure 28. Duncan used phrases from class contributions to create a free verse poem

Black line master on page 144

COMPARE/CONTRAST, GRADES 3-9

Resources

sheets of paper

Lon Po Po by Ed Young

The True Story of the Three Little Pigs by Jon Scieszka

Student Participation

Interp

LM

VL

VS

Purpose

This lesson challenges students by combining independent reading with content. The lesson teaches students a form for compare/contrast writing, using resource material that connects to their background experiences. The choice of cultural fairy tales reaffirms the importance of childhood stories and provides a forum for discussing cross-cultural aspects of these tales. Once the students understand how to work with the form, they more easily deal with challenging content and independent reading.

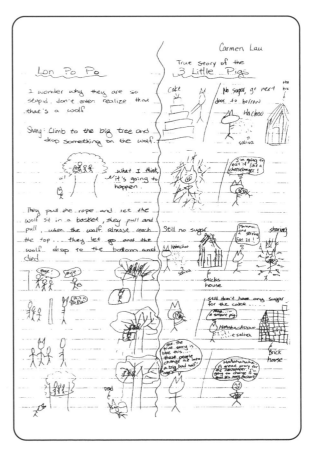

Figure 29. Carmen's comparison of two stories

The Process

1. Divide the class into heterogeneous groups of three or four students.

2. Give each member of the group a blank sheet of paper.

3. Have the students fold their sheet of paper in half lengthwise; one column is for each story. The students will record the plots in drawings or words after the texts are read.

4. Read each story aloud, showing the illustrations that accompany the text.

5. In their groups, have the students discuss the stories, identify similarities and differences, and record this information in the appropriate column on their sheets (see figure 29).

6. In a class discussion, create a master list of similarities and differences in the stories. Make sure each group contributes at least one idea (see figure 30).

7. Have each student write two paragraphs, comparing and contrasting the stories.

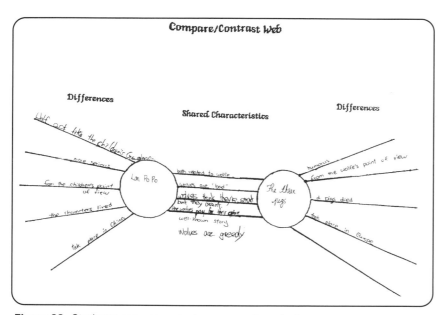

Figure 30. Students can use webs to compare two stories

USING MANIPULATIVES IN MATH, GRADES 4-9

Resources

black line master (see page 145)

pattern blocks (provide a set for each pair of students working together)

Student Participation

BK

VL

VS

LM

Interp

Purpose

Students are encouraged to use pattern blocks to develop, then demonstrate, several different ways a mathematical problem can be solved.

Many students who are learning English as a Second Language are able to work at their grade level or above in mathematics since they have learned how to complete numeric computations in their first languages. However, by asking these students to use manipulatives to *explain* their answer requires them to use language that describes their mathematical reasoning. Pattern blocks provide a concrete example from which to build language.

The Process

1. Divide the class into pairs of students.

2. Give each pair of students a set of pattern blocks.

3. Have the students work with the pattern blocks to determine how many of each shape there are (see figure 31). Explain that groupings of blue rhombuses, red trapezoids, and green triangles are equal to one yellow hexagon. While the students are working with the shapes, lead a class discussion about the fraction value of each of the shapes in reference to the hexagon. For example, one triangle equals one sixth of a hexagon.

4. After students have had an opportunity to explore the pattern blocks, have them use the blocks to reproduce the figure illustrated in the black line master (see figure 32).

5. Have students use the pattern blocks to determine what fraction of the figure is made up of rhombuses.

6. For students who complete the activity quickly, have them provide an oral explanation and a hands-on demonstration with the pattern blocks. (There are a number of ways to find the solution to this problem: the rhombuses make up 6/15 or 2/5 of the entire figure.)

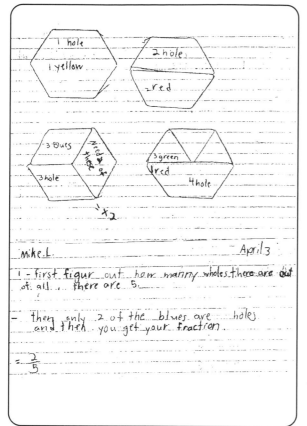

Figure 31. One student's solution to a math problem

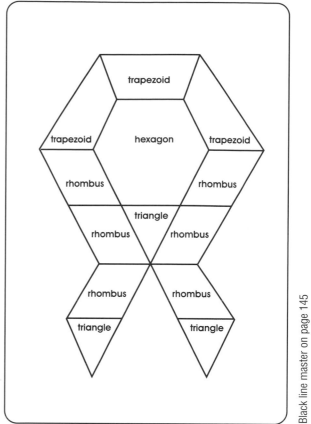

Figure 32. Students can use pattern blocks to reproduce this figure

Black line master on page 145

MANAGING TEXT WITH GRAPHICS, GRADES 4-9

Resources

text from science or social studies

graphic organizer

overhead projector

felt pen

Student Participation

VS

Interp

VL

LM

Purpose

After reading a passage of text, students are expected to understand the information they have read. While some students learning ESL may have knowledge of graphic organizers and how to work with them because charts, webs, and graphs are used in schools in other countries, many students will find it challenging to manage information in English.

This strategy involves teaching students to manage the information in texts by explicitly teaching them how to work with a passage of text. With a form for managing text under control, students can begin to write from the graphics they make, creating their own academic texts.

The Process

1. Read a passage from a social studies or science text aloud with the students.

2. Place a blank graphic on the overhead, and tell the students that the graphic is a tool for helping them manage the information in the text.

3. Label the graphic organizer chosen (e.g., web, diagram, compare/contrast chart, flow chart, classification tree, evaluation rating scale).

4. As a class, complete the graphic while reading the text.

5. Explicitly teach the students how to write using the information from the graphic you have developed together. Prompt the students with questions such as: What kind of graphic organizer is this? How does it help manage details in the text? How could we begin to write using the information in this graphic organizer?

6. Label the writing (e.g., Description), and direct the students' attention to the language appropriate to the task (the language of description).

7. When finished teaching how to write the text, read it aloud with the students.

8. Place students into groups of four.

9. Give each group of students a similar passage of text on a new topic. Have each group read the text, then complete a graphic to summarize the information in the text (see figure 33). Finally, have the students write their own text passage based on the graphic.

10. Establish criteria for evaluating. Students need to know specifically what is expected of them.

11. Have the students in each group present their graphic and an oral reading of their written text.

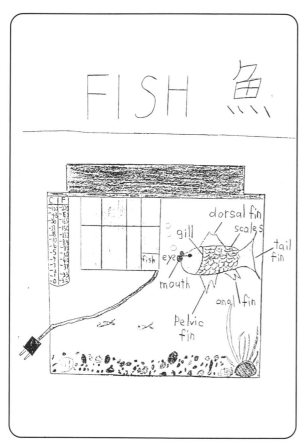

Figure 33. A group of students use a diagram to organize information from a text

CONCRETE EXPERIENCES: "REALIA" IN SOCIAL STUDIES, GRADES 4-9

Resources

realia (that reflect the people being studied)

black line master (see page 146)

Student Participation

BK

VS

VL

Interp

Purpose

The opportunities for creative thinking, vocabulary development, and problem solving are enhanced when students work together to investigate realia – authentic artifacts or reproductions of artifacts. The presentation of information as concrete experiences greatly assists ESL students because the materials are tangible. Even those with minimal English can find some aspect of the object to comment upon.

This strategy teaches students how to make careful observations of an object so that they can make some predictions about the group of people who used the artifact.

The Process

1. Assign students to heterogeneous groups.

2. Give each group a black line master (see figure 34) to use to guide discussions about the artifact.

THINKING LIKE AN ARCHAEOLOGIST

Look carefully at the object to determine:

- size, color, and weight
- materials it is made from
- way it was made
- any decoration on the object
- if it is ancient or modern

Uses:

- Possible uses of the object: for cooking, decoration, hunting, fishing, farming; for working, making music, religious purposes; as furniture; and so on
- Who might have used it? (e.g., farmers, city dwellers, artists, soldiers, students)
- Is such an object used today? Do you know of an object we use today that is similar?

Lifestyles:

- Would children, women, men, or the elderly have used this object?
- Where was it used? (e.g., indoors, rural or urban areas, outdoors)
- What might the object tell us about the lives of the people who used it? (e.g., work, leisure time, interests)
- What kind of people?
- Is it ancient or modern?

Based on our observations and discussion of this artifact, we believe that the artifact might have been used for: _____

by the _____ people.

Black line master on page 146

Figure 34. Groups of students use this form to record observations of an artifact

3. Present each group with an artifact to investigate.

4. Introduce the word *archaeologist*, and explain to the students that they are archaeologists for this exercise.

5. Give each group of "archaeologists" time to discuss and sketch the artifact.

6. Encourage students to record questions, observations, and vocabulary words used during the group's discussion around the sketch.

7. Have each group select a spokesperson to describe the group's observations about the artifact.

8. Give each group a "tip" about its artifact, which the "archaeologists" can then discuss.

9. Have the group members add any additional information and predictions to their observation sheets.

10. Have each student complete a Gallery Walk to view the other artifacts, then complete a web of information about what he/she has learned.

NARRATIVE WRITING FROM A VIDEO CLIP, GRADES 6-9

Resources

videos

sheets of paper

Student Participation

VL

VS

N

Interp

Purpose

When students view a short video clip they are presented with information through a familiar medium. When this information is recorded, a rich source of detail is available for them.

In this activity, students watch a video segment so that they can identify detail in the story specific to setting, characters, dialogue, and action. From this information, the students predict the outcome of the story. They then write a narrative composition in response, moving from the known (video as form and content) to the unknown.

The Process

1. Before introducing this lesson, preview several videos to find one that includes details about the setting and the characters who are involved in action and dialogue.

2. Prior to viewing the video as a class, have each student make a web that includes the following terminology: *setting, point of view, narrator, character, plot/action, conflict, climax,* and *dialogue.*

3. Have the students watch the video segment and record the information from the video on their webs simultaneously (see figure 35).

4. As they view the video, invite students to record their questions on the webs.

5. Have students watch the video segment again and add detail to the webs.

6. With a partner, have students ask questions, seek clarification, and compare notes. They can ask any remaining questions during class discussion.

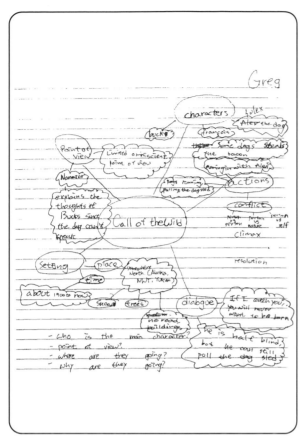

Figure 35. Greg filled in his web as he watched a video

7. Before the students start writing, have them use a comic book form to draw a plan for a narrative story that incorporates and builds upon the information contained in their webs.

8. After all students have had a chance to write down some of their ideas in a first draft (see figure 36), they can discuss their plot with a partner. Some students may want to share their ideas with the class.

9. Provide enough time for students to complete their first drafts.

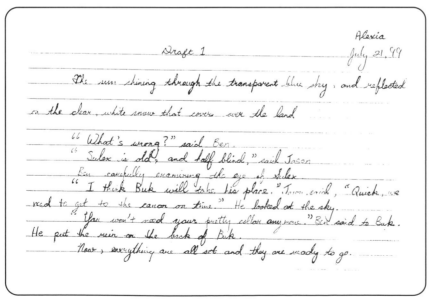

Figure 36. Alexia used information from her web in her first draft

UNIT PLANS

EXPLICITLY TEACHING ENGLISH THROUGH DAILY JOURNAL WRITING, GRADES 1-9

Introduction

Journal writing is a common activity in many classrooms. The purpose of journal writing is to use the students' personal experiences to support them as developing writers. However, asking ESL students (and, often, non-ESL students) to keep a daily journal without first providing them with models of writing can produce journals of little quality. ESL students are learning the language and need models. Teachers can explicitly model the writing process by keeping their own daily journal and sharing the entries with the students. In this way, the teacher's journal becomes the focus of instruction.

Daily journals can be used to monitor and teach ESL learners a wide variety of skills in written English. For example:

- how to write as a beginner
- vowel and consonant sounds in English (use any phonics book, create a word list to generate words)
- plurals
- past tense verbs
- past-present-future time
- ways of using more descriptive nouns
- steps in writing a procedure or directions
- criteria for marking writing
- how to write dialogue, poems, recipes
- how to edit

Daily journals have many benefits for supporting language learning in the classroom. Journals provide open-ended writing opportunities, so all students (ESL and non-ESL) can benefit from participation in journal writing. The common experience of journal writing and journal sharing helps build a community of learners in the classroom. Student progress is ensured with explicit teaching, high expectations, and ongoing monitoring of student progress.

- Journals provide physical evidence of an ESL student's growth in the English language.

- Journals can be used to motivate students when they are ready to give up and/or are struggling.

- Journals are a way of celebrating success in acquiring English, which is a difficult language to learn.

- Journals can be used to show parents/guardians how much has been accomplished over time.

- Journals can be helpful for identifying a particular area in which a student has difficulty with the English language. Teachers can then pay special attention to this area by planning some kind of intervention.

The Process

To begin, generate a list of topics.

Decide on a writing focus (e.g., plurals, vowel sounds, directions, descriptive adjectives), and write the teacher journal on the overhead or the chalkboard, incorporating the specific focus (see example Teacher Journal, page 182).

One day the journal is full of *a* sounding vowels: students can help make a list of them or underline the vowels with colored chalk or pen.

Another day the journal is full of past tense errors or the *s* is missing from plural words, and students have to add it. The teacher and students read aloud and hear the errors together. The teacher's work (not only theirs) needs editing.

Other days the teacher journal has exemplary long complex sentences in it (a model of good writing), and the students take the sentences apart.

The form of the writing varies from day to day. It can be a letter to a friend, a movie review, a poem, an ad, a dialogue from a scene in a play, a reflection on a school event. The options are as varied as are the lives of the students.

Reading the teacher's journal becomes a routine that all students enjoy. The "writing model" explicitly created by the teacher models correct forms of English in a nonthreatening way and is connected directly to reading. Students are motivated to read and write because they are excited to learn about the surprises that appear each day in the teacher's journal.

Step 1: At the start of the day, show the teacher journal to the students, and read aloud from it.

Step 2: As a class, read the journal entry aloud, and talk about the content of what has been written. Some skills to discuss might be:

- a word or two written in other languages

- spelling, correct use of grammar, additional words that could make the writing more interesting, how to create sentences that are increasingly complex, how to write an argument. The possibilities are limited only by the imaginations of the teachers and the students.

Step 3: The students write their own journal entry.

Beginning learners may write only one or two sentences in English, or they may write in a combination of English and the language of the home.

If learners do not know a word they want to use in their writing, explain that they have some options. They can (a) ask a classmate or the teacher for help, (b) draw the word, or (c) write the word in the first language and translate it when they have learned the word in English.

While spelling is not the focus of the daily journal, students will find that spelling comes more easily as they edit their work and learn to write. Students can sound words out, use emergent spelling, or leave a space when they come across a word they do not know. When they review their work, they can ask a classmate (first choice) or the teacher about the word. Often, they will learn from words that other students are spelling aloud.

Teacher Journal – Sample Lesson, Grades 1-3

Focus: Past tense verbs and words with an *s* sound

Journal Entry: Today, I came to school by car. It was raining cats and dogs and the roads were as slippery as a snake. I hope the sun shines tomorrow.

1. Show the entry on the overhead, or write it on the chalkboard.

2. Read the journal entry aloud.

3. Invite a few students to read the entry aloud individually or in pairs.

4. As a class, identify the focus words (past tense verbs and words with an *s* sound: *came, was, were; cats, dogs, roads, slippery, snake, sun, shines*).

5. Have a student circle all of the past tense verbs identified by the group.

6. Have another student circle all of the words with an *s* sound identified by the group.

7. Add other words with *s* sounds.

8. Ask students how to say the word *sun* in Cantonese, Japanese, Mandarin, Punjabi, Vietnamese, and Estonian.

Following this group activity, have students write in their own journals (or draw pictures if they have not any words yet; pictures can be transcribed by a teacher who circulates and supports writing). When finished, have each student read to a teacher and to a classmate of his/her choice (who is also finished writing). At the end of the lesson, have students hand in their journals. When reading the entries, write a positive comment in each student's journal. Add correct forms of words at the bottom of the page, never to correct the student but to provide a model and to teach editing skills over time. To extend students' writing and thinking, ask a question that the students can respond to the next day.

Step 4: Students read their journal entry to the teacher and a classmate of their choice. This activity gives ESL learners an opportunity to practice reading aloud in English.

Step 5: Collect all journals every day or every other day, read them, and initial the work.

When applicable, add a question at the bottom of a page and/or write correct forms of words in English in the margin (not to correct ESL learners but to add to the students' ideas).

Step 6: As the year progresses, the complexity of the work and the expectations for completion grow. The teacher and students collaborate to create criteria for submitting written work. Work submitted in journals is expected to adhere to the criteria agreed upon. Criteria may include:

■ statements about the length of written work

■ expectations for editing

- expectations for developing ideas
- expectations for giving details
- expectations for building skill at using English for writing

Step 7: Students keep their journals at school until the end of the year, and then the journals are sent home. Some teachers like to give each student a journal to record summer activities and travels in. The students bring their journals back to school in the fall.

Teacher Journal – Sample Lesson, Grades 4-9

Focus: Past tense verbs and a rating scale

Journal Entry: I watched a new video yesterday and wondered why it rated three stars. I found the plot boring and the special effects were not spectacular either. On a scale of one to ten, I would rate the plot a five and the special effects a six.

1. Display the entry on the overhead or the chalkboard.

2. Read the journal aloud with the class.

3. Have a few students read the entry aloud individually or in pairs.

4. Have a student circle all of the past tense verbs identified by the group (*watched, wondered, found, were*).

5. Discuss the idea of rating or ranking things such as videos, books, movies, and music.

6. Identify those words that indicate rating (*three stars, one to five, a five, a six*).

7. Add other words that suggest evaluation.

Following this group activity, have students write in their own journals, rating a video they have recently viewed. When they are finished, have each student read to the teacher and to a classmate of his/her choice who is also finished writing. When students hand in their journals, write a positive comment in each journal. To extend students' writing and thinking, ask a question that students can respond to the next day.

SCAFFOLDING EARLY READING AND WRITING, GRADE 1

(contributed by Joni Cunningham, Richmond, B.C., teacher)*

Introduction

Cracking into literacy requires time and interaction. Teaching literacy is most effective when experienced language users are available to scaffold with their language for the less experienced students.

In this unit, a different activity is planned for each day of the week to reinforce the "sounds" that are introduced on Monday. The students work with concrete, manipulative materials that allow them to maneuver and build words, not just listen, read, and write. This method engages young learners, and it reinforces Gardner's multiple intelligences theory.

The Process

The structure of the activity is as follows:

Friday

- Ask the students, with their families, to think of words on the weekend that begin with the next week's selected letter/sound (*m*, for example).

Monday

- As a class, brainstorm words that begin with the selected letter/sound. List the words on chart paper or the chalkboard.

- Have each student choose one word from the list that he/she wants to know how to read and spell by the end of the week.

- Write each selected word on Manila tag card, and give each student his/her card.

- Have each student make his/her word using five different manipulatives (for example, buttons, unifix cubes, pattern blocks, modeling clay, colored paper clips). In this way, each student builds and spells the word *five different times with five different materials*. (For students who do not need this activity, have them work on a writing activity such as a journal entry.)

Tuesday

- Have each student think of a sentence that includes his/her word.

- Write each sentence on Manila tag strip as each student dictates his/her sentence. To reinforce new vocabulary words, correct spelling, and different sentence arrangements, support the students in all possible ways.

---

* This way of supporting early readers and writers was first developed when Joni Cunningham, a grade 1-2 teacher, was challenged by the demographics of her student population. Approximately 70 percent of her students spoke a language other than English in their homes. Many of the other students in the class could also benefit from intensive literacy support.

- Give each student his/her sentence written on Manila tag strip. Have students read their sentence to six other students, who then initialize the back of the tag with a special blue marking pen. The six students can be chosen from those who are working on a journal entry (let these students know ahead of time that they will be asked to work as a responsive audience).

- To engage a large portion of the class in this instruction, it is critical to work with additional support staff (for example, English language support teacher, parent helper, teaching assistant, or even an older student who could benefit from providing leadership to younger students).

Wednesday

- Have each student again read his/her sentence, this time to one person and/or the teacher, and then cut the sentence into words.

- Have the student read each word to another student (one of the "original six"), who then initializes each word in red. This activity encourages students to read words that are out of context.

- Have the students reconstruct their sentence, have it verified that the words are in the correct order, then tape the words, in the proper order, into their journal.

Grade-one students copy their sentence several times into their journal, as a draft or on newsprint underneath the taped words. By February, the grade-one students also begin to generate one of their own sentences.

Grade-two students use their sentence as their "topic sentence," and they continue to draft sentences about it. By January, these students are drafting three more sentences (begin by having them add just one more sentence).

Thursday

- Explain that Thursday is "edit day." Conference with each student individually, and edit and proofread his/her writing. (Having two teachers involved in the activity greatly assists the process.)

- Explain to the students that by January they will be working in small editing groups so that they learn to assume the editing and proofreading roles independently.

Friday

- Have students illustrate their final draft.

- Engage students in a constant review of their own writing. Have a teaching assistant ask students to read both old and new sentences from their journals. Repeated reading of their own writing assists students' literacy development.

CINDERELLA RETOLD: USING MULTICULTURAL STORIES, GRADES 2-5

Introduction

We set out to teach a unit* with a multicultural focus that integrated drama and language development.

Our school had been amassing a collection of Cinderella tales that represented many different cultures. The purposes of the collection were to (1) provide students with opportunities to learn about cultural diversity and develop acceptance of differences, and (2) encourage positive self-esteem for all students.

We decided to use the Cinderella tales as the "hook" for the unit. Most of our students were familiar with the story of Cinderella. For those who were not, the similarities in the plot line of each tale would help them comprehend the main events.

Our goals included:

- Have students identify the beginning, middle, and ending of the tale through reinforcing the basic structure for storytelling. Students could then transfer these skills to their own story compositions.

- Provide ESL beginners with opportunities to work with English-speaking classmates. A variety of reading, writing, speaking, and listening activities would be used to enhance communication skills in English.

- Assist students in appreciating these stories from a multicultural perspective. Embedded in the language and the illustrations in each book was rich information from which the students could learn more about the cultural groups represented in the stories.

- Have the students write and perform a play based on their Cinderella fairy tale.

The Process

Day 1

- Divide the class into groups of three or four students. Ensure that each group has a developed English speaker and a student who is learning English.

- Have each teacher on the team read multicultural Cinderella stories to prepare for the first lesson. (We chose to read six versions.)

- Record the stories on cassette tapes so that the students can listen to the stories anytime they need to during this unit.

---

* The combined grade 2/3 class for which this unit was originally developed comprised of approximately 40 percent ESL students. The unit represents a collaboration in planning and teaching between the English language support teacher and the classroom teacher. All activities, however, are possible when working alone in the classroom or in a separate ESL setting.

- Make brief notes about the plot, interesting cultural traditions, and the characters in each story for the book talk (a brief chat about the book to interest the students).

- Following the book talks, give each group an opportunity to look through the various renditions of the Cinderella story to decide which two books the students in the group find the most interesting.*

- Have the students come to a group consensus and write down their first choice and second choice with details explaining their first choice.

   If two groups select the same first choice, look at their explanations before deciding which group will have first choice.

> **Cinderella Unit**
>
> Group members:
>
> Our first choice of Cinderella stories is:
>
> This story is our first choice because:
>
> Our second choice is:

Day 2

- Assign a different version of the Cinderella story to each group, based on the information that each group submitted.

- Have the groups listen to their story on cassette while following the story in their book.

Day 3

- Prepare a large pie chart with eight sections on 11 x 17-inch paper. On the outside of the pie chart, write the words, *Beginning, Middle,* and *Ending* to remind students of chronological events in the story that correspond with each of the three sections. Make a copy for each group.

- Involve the students in a discussion of the story to determine the main events.

- Distribute one copy of the chart to each group of students, and have the groups complete the chart with both a written description of the events and an illustration (see figure 37).

Day 4

- Distribute a pie chart to each student (see black line master page 147).

- Display the group pie charts in the classroom to remind students of the events in the story. Some ESL learners may want to listen to the story again. Other students can join them in listening to the tape, looking at the illustrations, or rereading the text.

- Assist students in making connections between the story and the illustrations in the text.

---

* Various multicultural versions of Cinderella are listed in Children's Literature on page 167.

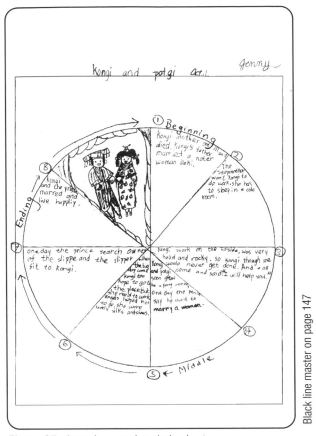

Kongi and potgi act.1   Jenny

① Beginning
Kongi mother sk
died. Kongi's father
married a noter
woman Dah.

② The
steopmother
want kongi to
do work. she has
to sleep in a cold
room.

⑧ Ending
Kongi
and the pr
marred and
live happily.

③ kongi work on the hillside, was very
hard and rocky. so kongi though she
would never get done. And a ox
and potgi come and said "I will help you."

⑦ one day the prince search ow ne
of the slippe and the slipper when
fit to kongi.   the big kongi too Soon grow
            day come
            kongi too
            hope to go to be a young worm
            the place but one day the prince
            she need to work say he want to
            angels helped her marry a woman.
            to go. she wore
            lovely silks and shoes.

⑥

⑤ ← Middle

④

Black line master on page 147

Figure 37. Jenny's completed pie chart

Day 5

■ Link to the social studies curriculum: have students look at a large map of the world and locate where they live and the country in which their story is set.

■ Distribute a small map of the world to all students, and have them transfer the information from the large map to their map (for reference). Support students by helping them identify places on the large-scale map. Encourage ESL students to show their map skills by helping others locate their birth countries on the map.

Day 6

■ As a class, develop an organizational chart about the people and the country from which each story originates. Distribute an 11 x 17-inch version of the chart to each student (see black line master page 148).

■ Gather encyclopedias and books that focus on both the people and land of each country to augment the information in each story. Use encyclopedias that are highly visual with maps, photos, and captions to assist less able readers make predictions based on what they see.

■ Move from group to group, and support students in their use of the reference materials (see figure 38).

■ Encourage groups to actively involve all members in a positive way.

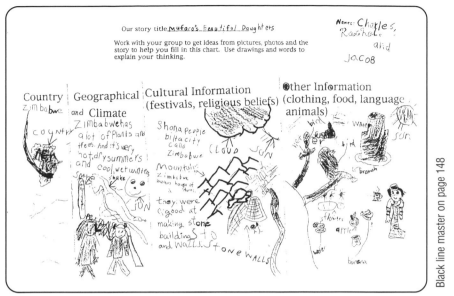

Figure 38. One group organized the information from *Mufaro's Beautiful Daughters*

Note: Students in one of our groups invited a Korean student to tell them the name of a traditional Korean outfit that they had seen in the encyclopedia and the story behind the outfit. The student gave them the word in both English and Korean and wrote out both versions. She was very proud that she was sought out as an expert on Korean culture!

Day 7

■ Have each student create a sociogram chart (see figure 39). A sociogram is used to describe the way that the main characters in the story interact with one another. The sociogram can contain words from brainstorming sessions or new language vocabulary heard during group discussions.

■ As a class, brainstorm words that describe the relationship between the Cinderella character and her stepmother. Encourage students to think about both sides of the relationship: Cinderella's feelings about her stepmother and the stepmother's feelings about Cinderella.

■ In their groups, have the students discuss the main characters and their relationships with one another.

The sociogram chart and group discussions are key activities in helping students understand each character's point of view and what motivates him/her. Circulate among the groups as students are completing their sociograms, and offer assistance whenever necessary. Have students explain why they think a character responded to another character in the way described in their sociogram.

Day 8

■ With each group, review the main events of the Cinderella story the students worked on.

■ Join in the group discussions of the plot in terms of beginning, middle, and ending events. Ensure that one student in the group is recording the information. For ESL students, this is another great opportunity for them to review the main events in the story.

- Explain to students that they are now going to create a tableaux, which consists of a series of "frozen poses" representing scenes from the story. This activity provides an opportunity for students to show their knowledge of the story using a nonverbal representation.

Days 9 and 10

- As a class, discuss the importance of working together to choose pivotal events in the story. Have students represent the events they have chosen using gesture, body position, and facial expression.

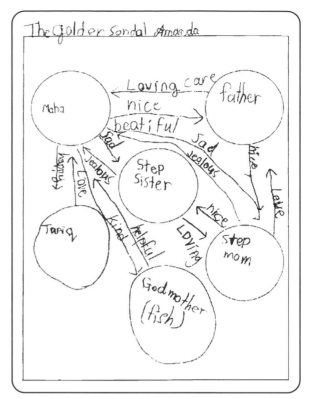

Figure 39. Amanda's sociogram chart

- Teach students that from an audience's perspective, *tableaux* are most effective when the actors use varying heights, from floor level to standing, to show a scene.

- As a class, generate criteria for the tableaux with the students.

- Before students present their tableaux, have them explain to the audience each of their scenes and indicate which character they will play.

- Have the students in each group make a presentation of their tableaux.

Criteria generated with our students:

- show three "frozen pictures" to represent the beginning, middle, and end of the story
- all actors face the audience and are frozen in position
- all actors use facial expressions to express emotion
- all students in the group work cooperatively

Rating:

Powerful: the group goes beyond all of the criteria

Competent: most of the criteria are met

Developing: some of the criteria are met

Days 11 and 12

- Students are now ready to write a script for their Cinderella story. Teach a mini-lesson to prepare the students: outline how to use dialogue and a narrator to develop the plot.

- Support students by showing them how to maintain a consistent voice throughout the script and by encouraging them to not include too much detail.

- At this point, teacher intervention should be minimal – students should be used to working cooperatively and inclusively while sharing the task of writing.

- Encourage students in each group to assist their classmates who are learning English by modeling structurally and grammatically correct sentences.

- Encourage the quieter members of each group to contribute their ideas.

- When the group has finished a first draft of the script, the members read the script orally and discuss whether or not ideas need to be added or deleted.

- Keyboard each script into a computer, then photocopy the scripts so that the groups can practice their plays.

- Have students list and plan for the props and the costumes they will need. Give them time to gather costumes and construct props.

- As a class, determine the criteria for rating the plays.

Days 13-16

- Give students time to select their parts, learn their lines, and rehearse.

- Coach the students in effective use of voice, articulation, action, physical location, and facial expression.

- Encourage students to coach each other using Praise, Questions, and Suggestions (P. Q. S.). Model prompts for the students:

  - "I liked the part when..."

  - "I noticed that..."

  - "I wondered why..."

- Send a letter home with each student inviting parents to join the audience.

- Arrange to have a parent videotape each play.

Day 17

- Have the students in each group present their play. Have the remaining students watch each play and complete the evaluation form (see figure 40).

Criteria for the Plays

- the cultural group is represented through the costumes or the script
- appropriate actions and facial expressions are used
- speech is clear and enhances the role
- a cooperative effort is demonstrated
- actors know their parts and remain in character
- members of the audience demonstrate attentive skills

Rating:

Powerful: the group goes beyond all of the criteria

Competent: most of the criteria are met

Developing: some of the criteria are met

Day 18

- Have students reflect in their journals on the experience of this unit of study.

As teachers, we found this unit of study very worthwhile. The growth of the ESL students' communication skills was outstanding, and the class became a tight-knit community. All students demonstrated increased proficiency using story structures beginning, middle, and end in both reading and writing.

MULTICULTURAL CINDERELLA PLAYS

Name:______________________________

One thing I noticed about each play:

a. ____

____

b. ____

____

c. ____

____

d. ____

____

e. ____

____

Cultural Information included in our play

Country: ____

Customs: ____

____

____

____

Black line master on page 149

Figure 40. Student Evaluation form

THE ENCHANTED ANKLET

Setting:	Cindurinagar, India
Characters:	Cinduri, Stepmother, Stepsister, Prince, Godfather Snake
Narrator:	Cinduri's parents died so she was left to depend on her stepmother. Her stepmother makes Cinduri go to the lake to get water. Cinduri must also cook, get vegetables, and do many other chores.
Stepmother:	Do your chores now Cinduri!
Cenduri:	Yes, stepmother. Whatever you say.
Stepsister:	Wash my dresses.
Stepmother:	Did you do your chores?
Cinduri:	Yes, stepmother, all of my chores are done.
Narrator:	One day when Cinduri is at the lake gathering water, she sees a snake with a jewel on its head.
Godfather:	I will be your Godfather for ever.
Cinduri:	Thank you very, very much. That's wonderful.
Stepmother:	We are going to the Navaratri Festival but you cannot go. You have to do your work on the farm.
Narrator:	Cinduri is disappointed so she goes to find her Godfather snake.
Cinduri:	Please help me go to the festival.
Godfather:	Take this jewel. Rub the jewel and make a wish. (She rubs the jewel.)
Narrator:	Cinduri's old rags magically turned into a beautiful sari. She went to the festival and there everyone thought that she was beautiful.
Prince:	Would you dance with me?
Cinduri:	Of course your highness. I'd be honored.
Narrator:	Cinduri had to leave the festival early and she lost the anklet on the doorstep.
Prince:	Wait! How will I find you? I don't even know your name. (The prince picks up the anklet.)
Prince:	I will find the girl who owns this anklet. Whoever fits the anklet is the girl whom I will marry.
Narrator:	Many young women try on the anklet but it does not fit them, The prince finally arrives at Cinduri's house.
Prince:	I want you girls to try on this anklet. (The stepsister tries on the anklet but it doesn't fit.)
Prince:	(speaking to Cinduri) Would you like to try on the anklet?
Cinduri:	Of course I would your highness.
Narrator:	Cinduri tried on the anklet and it fit perfectly. The Prince and Cinduri were married that very day.

Black line master on page 150

Figure 41. Sample of a student script, based on the book *The Enchanted Anklet*

INDIVIDUAL NOVEL STUDIES, GRADES 4-9

Introduction

Teaching about novels to students who are at a range of proficiency levels in mastering English can present considerable challenges. While the teacher can select a novel that is grade and age appropriate, the novel still may not be accessible to many students in the class. One solution is to develop a collection of activities that challenges and interests all students, then let students choose their own novels. This is possible because there are common elements to all novels. These include characters, settings, plot, problem/ resolution, and climax.

The activities need to be open-ended so that beginners in English can read novels that are high interest and low vocabulary, participate fully in the activities, and develop their English. At the same time, students who are more advanced or proficient in English can work with complex novels and participate in the same activities at an appropriate level of challenge. When they work with open-ended activities, all students are engaged in thinking and in constructing an understanding – regardless of the complexity of the text or of their English proficiency.

During individual novel studies, teachers can move around the classroom and spend time with every student. As student expertise with an activity develops, the teacher team can add an additional activity (e.g., compare/ contrast two or more characters, identify and describe the protagonist, look for and create similes or metaphors). After a time, students may be asked to choose five or six activities from ten possible choices. The quantity of activities in the collection is limitless. What is important is that students are not just being assigned activities, they are being *taught* how to work proficiently with each activity.

The activities provide a shared context for teaching and learning. Teachers teach each activity, then students apply the activity to the novel they have chosen. This meets the demands offered by diverse groups of learners.

We have used the following activities successfully many times with diverse groups of students across a variety of grade levels. When students use this approach, rather than work as a whole class on the same novel, they read far more, are more enthusiastic and engaged, and demonstrate more sophisticated reading behaviors.

The Process

Before students select their novel, either from the school library or a classroom library collection, develop criteria for selecting the individual novels. Criteria may include novels that are:

- reasonable length
- high quality
- challenging

- right level of difficulty
- variety of types or genres (e.g., fiction, nonfiction, adventure, and fantasy)

Share criteria information with the students to ensure that everyone understands how to select an appropriate novel for study. Encourage students to select novels that are culturally diverse. Such novels will help them learn different ideas about people and places and offer them an opportunity to develop their knowledge of the world and its diversity.

Students who choose the same novel can work in partners. Working with a partner can be particularly advantageous to the students learning English as a second language – conversations between partners will support their developing comprehension and English skills. Provide students with class time to read their novel, as well as the time to do the writing activities.

Modeling the Activity

- Model the activity with a pre-selected book.
- Encourage students to make predictions about the book based on the illustrations and information on the book cover.
- Record the predictions on a web (use felt markers and large print).
- Develop the criteria for evaluation with the students.

The Activity: Part 1

- Have each student select the novel he/she wants to read.
- Give students time lines for completing their reading and their written work.
- Encourage students to take books and written activities home for additional work.
- Introduce the activity that models a title page (see figure 42a).
- Have the students complete the sheet using information from their novels.

Note: Beginners can draw their predictions or write some words in their first languages until they have developed enough English to participate fully. Intermediate and advanced students have an opportunity to work to the level of challenge that is appropriate.

Figure 42a. Title page for novel studies

INDIVIDUAL NOVEL STUDY

Name. _____

Grade: _____

Date: _____

Title of novel:

_____

Author:

_____

Type of novel (for example, fiction, adventure):

_____

My predictions about the novel – I think this story is about:

Consider who, where, what, why, when, and how.

The Activity: Part 2

Model the activity sheet that involves character (see figure 42b) as follows:

- Enlarge the sheet or make an overhead of it, and work with the students to complete all of the activities together.

- To scaffold the activity for beginners, role-play the chosen character from the pre-selected novel. For these students, the experience will be concrete, immediate, and shared. For other students, select a passage from a novel of their choice that is about a character. Make an overhead of the passage, and have the students web the details as you work through the description of the character.

- To explicitly teach students how to think about the information as you organize it on the web, have them add their ideas to the web on their activity sheet as the ideas are generated.

- With the information on the web, model how to write a description of a character.

- As a class, create criteria for marking. In this example, the criteria include assigning marks for:

  - detailed web

  - written passage of appropriate length and quality

  - organization

  - use of descriptive adjectives or adverbs

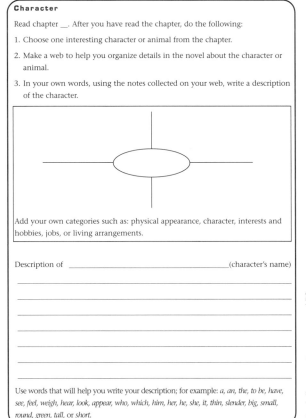

Character

Read chapter __. After you have read the chapter, do the following:

1. Choose one interesting character or animal from the chapter.

2. Make a web to help you organize details in the novel about the character or animal.

3. In your own words, using the notes collected on your web, write a description of the character.

Add your own categories such as: physical appearance, character, interests and hobbies, jobs, or living arrangements.

Description of _____ (character's name)

Use words that will help you write your description; for example: *a, an, the, to be, have, see, feel, weigh, hear, look, appear, who, which, him, her, he, she, it, thin, slender, big, small, round, green, tall,* or *short.*

Figure 42b. Character page for novel studies

Black line master on page 152

- Establish a time line for completing the work.

- Have students work individually or in partners to complete the character activity. Advanced students may work on more than one character, or they may add lined sheets for longer written work. Beginners may start with a few items and sentences but will build their skills over time.

As the quality of students' work increases, so do the expectations of their work. For the next novel study, for example, students might be required to make predictions with greater details or imagination to obtain the same marks. Or they may be asked to write a paragraph that summarizes their predictions about the novel.

Teaching the Activities

The teaching process for all remaining activities – setting, time line, illustrated action strip, choosing and decision making, and evaluating the novel – is the same (see figure 42c).

- Use a pre-selected novel or a paragraph from another novel to teach the activity sheet explicitly.

- Enlarge the activity sheets or make overheads, and work with the students to complete all of the components together.

- Collaboratively create marking criteria with the students.

- Establish time lines for completing work.

Reading rates vary and so will the times that students need to complete the activities on their own. This is not a problem: when a student is finished reading the novel and has completed the written activities, he/she starts another novel. Proficient readers can often complete two novels and the activities in the time it takes some beginning ESL learners to complete one novel. This is an example of adapting the reading material, the time it takes to complete the activity, and the amount of work that is completed.

- Have students submit their novel study for marking, or evaluate the study together with the student. After each novel study, conference with each student and set goals for improving the quality of his/her work.

Setting

Draw the setting (place, location, or scene that interests you) from chapter __. Then, write to describe the setting you have illustrated. Be sure to include details in your writing.

Drawing of the setting in chapter __.

Description of _____

_____

_____

_____

_____

_____

_____

Use words that will help you write your descrip

see, feel, weigh, hear, look, appear, who, which, hin

round, green, tall, or *short.*

Time Line

Organize the important events in chapter __ in a sequence on the time line from the beginning of the action to the end of the action. Then, use your time line to write the events in the order that they occurred.

Put the action in time order.

_____ chapters:

_____

_____

_____

_____

_____

p you write about the events; for example:

next, second, third, last, after, finally, at the end,

below, over/under, next to, between, in front of,

Illustrated Action Strip

1. Choose several scenes from your time line.

2. Decide which scene represents the problem, the climax or most important moment, and the resolution or the way the problem was solved.

3. Illustrate each scene with drawings and words.

Scenes

Climax

Problem or Conflict

Resolution

Use language of action/consequences/reaction to help you; for example: *is caused by, is the result of, is a consequence of, because, is probably, most likely, predict, forecast,* or *if/then.*

Choosing and Decision Making

1. Write about or illustrate the problem or

2. Write about or illustrate the resolution t

3. On a decision-making diagram, organize another option.

Problem and/or conflict in the novel:

Choices and decisions made by the charact

Decision-Making Diagram

decision or choice

problem or conflict

decision or choice

Use language that will help you write about choices; for example: *can, will, may, might, could, to decide, to choose, to take,* or *to select.*

in the novel you have read for evaluation.

nized to write an evaluation of the novel.

		ory	Good	Very Good	Excellent	Outstanding
			4	5	6	7

Evaluation of the novel: _____

_____

_____

_____

_____

_____

_____

Use words that help you write your evaluation; for example: *to rank, to evaluate, to believe, to value, to analyze, good/better/best, satisfactory/unsatisfactory, right/wrong,* or *good/evil.*

Figure 42c. Remaining activity pages for novel studies

Black line masters on pages 153-157

WRITING A CURRENT EVENTS ESSAY, GRADES 6-9

Introduction

One assumption sometimes made is that by the time students are in secondary school they can organize their ideas well enough to compose clearly written essays. It is our experience that students need to be taught a specific essay structure before they can write an essay. Teaching essay writing is invaluable for students who are learning English and for native-English-speaking students. Good expository writing requires lots of practice with built-in teacher support throughout the writing process.

Plagiarism can be a problem with beginning ESL students who are learning to write expository passages. Giving students an outline of what to include in each paragraph can help alleviate this. Each subtopic is developed in the space of a single paragraph, which requires students to synthesize the information they read and to rewrite the ideas in a concise way. This exercise also provides an opportunity to teach students how to use quotes from "experts" in a way that gives credit to the original author.

The Process

We gather a variety of newspapers, both local and national, for a two-week period. From these papers, we select several news stories that are ongoing rather than short lived.

The following mini-lessons are designed to be taught in approximately fifteen to twenty minutes during English class. Students can be given class time to practice or they can do the lessons as homework. Since gathering articles is completed over a period of time, this series of skills is taught as a sequence of lessons. This enables the students to learn a skill and practice it before a new skill in the sequence is introduced. Students receive support during this process to ensure that they are on track with the skills being taught; extra support is provided as needed.

A systematic plan is needed to teach students how to write an essay. For the first assignment the following parts of the essay are the focus:

- subtopics
- use of facts and quotes
- introductory and concluding paragraphs

The evaluation includes specific criteria for each paragraph. Students are more likely to practice certain writing skills if they are awarded marks each time they use a skill.

Day 1

- Give the students the details of the essay and the outline for the five paragraphs that they will write (see figures 43 and 44).
- Have students browse through the newspapers to see the kinds of articles that are currently in the news.

INVESTIGATING A CURRENT STORY IN THE NEWS

Choose an ongoing story in the news and collect all the articles and information that you can find on that topic. You will need a minimum of five different articles. Record the date of each article and the source in which the article was found. For those of you who are able to read newspapers or magazines in a language other than English, include a short translation of the main ideas in the article.

The key will be to choose a topic that interests you. You will be reading newspapers and magazines for several weeks to gather information about your topic. Before you start to collect articles, you must see me to approve your topic.

Remember, this is an ongoing assignment, and it cannot be completed in a few days.

You will be evaluated on the following components:

1. Organization of the articles as outlined above.
2. A summary of the articles written as an expository essay (a detailed outline will be provided for you to follow).
3. Your conclusions, based on what you have read on your chosen topic.

Black line master on page 158

Figure 43. Investigating a current news story

INVESTIGATING A CURRENT STORY IN THE NEWS: ESSAY OUTLINE

After you have collected news articles on your topic, reread each article and highlight ideas that you have identified as being important. Follow this outline for the paragraphs required in the essay.

(a) Paragraph 1

- introductory paragraph: introduces the reader to your topic and to the *three subtopics* to be discussed in the essay

(b) Paragraph 2

- introductory sentence: the first subtopic (explain this in detail)
- include an example from your news articles that gives more information about the subtopic (a quotation from the article could be used as a supporting statement)
- explain your example clearly

(c) Paragraph 3

- introductory sentence: the second subtopic
- use an example from one of the articles
- explain your example clearly

(d) Paragraph 4

- introductory sentence: the third subtopic
- use an example from one of the articles
- explain your example clearly

(e) Paragraph 5

- include the central ideas from paragraphs 2 through 4
- include the consequences of your findings
- include your predictions for the future

The final draft of the essay should be approximately one page in length.

Black line master on page 159

Figure 44. Current news story: essay outline

- Have students search for a topic at home by reading newspapers, news magazines, and articles on the Internet.
- Give students two days to determine their topic.

Day 2

- Hold a short conference with the students to help them decide on their topics. Students sometimes struggle with an inappropriate topic – one that is too big ("murders") or one that is too specific ("a car accident").
- If a student has a hard time choosing a topic, refer him/her to examples of topics that could be developed.

Day 3

- After the topics chosen by the students have been approved by the teacher, have students continue to collect articles and bring them to class.
- Have students organize the articles by gluing them next to a bibliography-style reference in a scrapbook or by arranging the articles in an assignment folder.
- Encourage students who are researching similar topics to meet and discuss the articles that they have collected.

Day 4

- To model the activity, share a pre-selected topic with the students: use a web format to introduce three subtopics for the essay. (A topic we used was the "runaway" film productions that are being filmed in Canada rather than in the United States.)

- Have the students read their articles and identify three subtitles related to their essay topic.

> **Example: Runaway film productions**
>
> subtopic 1
>
> - reasons why US film and TV productions are being filmed in Canada
>
> subtopic 2
>
> - for the Canadian film industry more work = more revenue
>
> subtopic 3
>
> - US film workers and their concerns about "runaway productions"

Day 5

- Display the articles on the overhead projector, and use colored highlighter pens to show supporting facts and details for each of the three subtopics. Explain that highlighter pens add a visual means for organizing the facts and details of each subtopic.

- Have the students use colored highlighter pens to show facts and details that support each of their subtopics.

Day 6

- Model ways to embed a quote in a sentence.

- Have students find quotes that support each subtopic.

Day 7

- Discuss and model the introductory paragraph.

Day 8

- Discuss and model the concluding paragraph as it appears in the essay outline. Students then begin the process of writing their essays following the outline provided.

Day 9

- Give students an evaluation sheet so that they can do a self-evaluation of their essay (see figure 45).

- Have students exchange essays with a partner who will also complete an evaluation of the essay.

- Have students hand in their completed evaluation sheet with the essay attached for evaluation.

When we evaluate the essays we look for evidence that the student has included each of the components listed in the essay outline. At this point we are more concerned that the students are able to organize their ideas coherently into paragraphs than we are with syntax and grammatically correct sentences. We do a small edit of the more glaring syntactical and grammatical errors, but our goal is to get the students to practice the writing skills they have learned during this process (see figures 46 and 47). Once the students understand the basic structure of the essay, we concentrate on the sentences that convey the information to the reader.

NEWS ESSAY SELF-EVALUATION SHEET

Reread your essay for the purpose of self-evaluation. Give yourself marks for including the following components:

Introduction/Paragraph 1
- explanation of the new story in an introductory sentence /1 mark
- the three subtopics in the essay are introduced /1 mark

Paragraph 2
- the first subtopic is included /1 mark
- one example is given explaining the subtopic /1 mark
- one quote or reference is included /1 mark

Paragraph 3
- the second subtopic is included /1 mark
- one example is given explaining the subtopic /1 mark
- one quote or reference is included /1 mark

Paragraph 4
- the third subtopic is included /1 mark
- one example is given explaining the subtopic /1 mark
- one quote or reference is included /1 mark

Paragraph 5
- a concluding statement about the topic is included /1 mark
- a summary of the main points is made /1 mark
- a statement about future considerations is included /1 mark

Once you have completed the self-evaluation, exchange essays and evaluation sheets with a partner to check that you are both in agreement with the marks given for each other's essay. Try to reach a consensus about the mark. Your signatures will indicate that both of you agreed with the mark given for this essay.

Essay mark /14   Signature: _____
(student)   author

Essay mark /14   Signature: _____
(teacher)   reader

Black line master on page 160

Figure 45. Students complete a self-evaluation of their news essay

---

CANADIAN HOCKEY TEAM THREATENING TO MOVE SOUTH OF THE BORDER

The Canadian hockey teams' owners had finally ask the federal government for help. The high player salaries, high taxation and Canadian citizens begin to lose interest on hockey are three main reason why Canadian owners are planning to move their teams to United States. On June 29th, 1999, all six Canadian hockey franchises sent one representative to meet with the Industry Minister John Manley, they hoped they could find a way to rescue these struggling hockey teams.

Thanks to the "Mighty American owners", the average National Hockey League salary had been raised from $270,000 eight years ago to $1.2 million U.S today. Small market cities like Calgary and Edmonton just can not afford those high-price players, that lead to millions and millions lost because fans are not interested in watching these "pretenders". Even the Montreal Canadiens are having trouble selling tickets. "The problem is the market price for players doesn't seem to have any control..." analyzed Canadiens assistant coach Dave King.

"My impression is...we will be able to work out something over the next several weeks that will go a long way to an overall solution," Said Ottawa Senators owner Rod Bryden after the day-long meeting. "We can be part of the solution, but the problem is really a taxation problem; it is not a players problem," Said Bob Goodenow, executive director of the National Hockey League Players Association. Combined, the six teams lost $170 million over the 1996-97 and 1996-98 seasons, largely because of the $220 million tax bill the six franchises face from all levels of government. Reducing property and sales taxes, an onerous entertainment tax in some provinces and a low Canadian dollar will be discuss in the negotiation between the two sides.

Due to "the coolest game on earth" become "the lowest scoring game on earth" and Canadian based hockey team losing competitiveness, hockey fans in Canada are starting to lose interest to the game. According to FOXTV ratings for the 1998 All-Star game in Vancouver were among the worst for any major league sports event in American TV history.

Will the federal government rescue these hockey teams' owners? Think about it. Will the public agree to give these "millionaires" a help instead of helping those leaky condomania owners who spent their life-time saving on a "watermania". If there is nothing done by the next five or six years, we could probably see all the remaining teams follow the footstep of the Winnipeg Jets and the Quebec Northiques who move south in recent years. By then, we might be watching All American Hockey Association instead of National Hockey League on the television.

Figure 46. Keith's essay

ONGOING NEWS STORY
ESSAY EVALUATION

Reread your essay for the purpose of self-evaluation. Give yourself marks for the following components:

Introduction/Paragraph 1
-explanation of the news stories in an introductory sentence /1 mark
-three topics that are covered in the essay are introduced /1 mark

Paragraph 2
-first topic included /1 mark
-one example of this topic /1 mark
-one quote or reference used /1 mark

Paragraph 3
-second topic included /1 mark
-one example of this topic /1 mark
-one quote or reference used /1 mark

Paragraph 4
-third topic included /1 mark
-one example of this topic /1 mark
-one quote or reference used /1 mark

Paragraph 5
-included a concluding statement about the topic /1 mark
- future considerations /1
-summary /1.5

Once you have completed the self evaluation, swap essays and evaluation sheets with a partner to check that you are both in agreement with the marks given for each other's essays. If there is a disagreement then you must reach an agreement through discussion. You and your partner must sign below to indicate that the mark given is fair and agreed upon.

Student Total: 13.9/14   Teacher Total: 14/14

Signatures: _____   _____
                    author   reader

Keith, you've written a very clear essay about the current problems for Canadian NHL teams. Make sure that you write using your language instead of another author's language eg "onerous entertainment tax". Why do you think that people are not paying for tickets at hockey games?

Figure 47. The teacher added comments to Keith's essay self-evaluation

APPENDIX

BLACK LINE MASTERS

Welcome to_____School.

This is a drawing of my school.

School Address:_____

Phone Number:_____

Fax Number: _____

Web Site/E-mail:_____

My name:_____

My grade:_____

My teacher:_____

My room number:_____

FIGURE 1 (pages 22-23) • **105**

I visited the office.

_____ is the principal.

_____ is the secretary.

They gave me this:

Some of the things I saw in the office are:

I visited the library.

_____ is the librarian.

Some of the things I saw in the library are:

I got this in the library:

FIGURE 1 (CONT'D) • 107

I saw some of the classrooms.

Room Number	Grade	Teacher

_____ gave me this:

Some of the things I really liked in the classrooms I saw are:

I found the washroom
closest to my classroom.

(draw what you saw)

I found the water fountain.

(draw what you saw)

I saw the gym.

(draw what you saw)

I saw the lunch area.

(draw what you saw)

I found the playground.

(draw what you saw)

The nurse is_____.

The counselor is_____.

FIGURE 1 (CONT'D) • 109

All About Me

This is a drawing of me and my family.

My name in English is _____.

My name in another language is _____.

This is something I left behind when I came to this school.

This was my old home, and this is
a drawing of my new home.

This is a drawing of my old school, and this is my
new school.

FIGURE 1 (CONT'D) • 111

I am _____ years old, and my birthday is on _____.

I can _____.

I came to this school from _____.

I can speak _____, and I will learn English.

This is a drawing of some of the things I like:

Wired to Buy

Have you heard of Generation Y, the Digital Generation, the Millennials, or the Echo Boomers? If you have not yet, you will very soon. Many executives in the corporate world of advertising are studying and surveying the habits and interests of the 78 million young people who have been born since 1978. By the year 2010, it is estimated that the population of teenagers will peak at 35 million! Such a large group of consumers has the corporate world trying to learn more about what teens want to buy.

Teens today are believed to have approximately 25 percent more income than teenagers did five years ago. It is well known that teens spend billions of dollars a year on clothes, and many of them use a credit card for those purchases. Advertisers are also aware that this generation of teens is the first computer-literate group of shoppers.

Today's teens are very used to seeing advertising, and they identify with specific brand names. Catalogs (in both print and computer formats) have been developed for teens to capitalize on their buying power. In addition to showing a selection of items that can be purchased, some of these catalogs include articles that highlight fashion news, health information, and advice about relationships. The on-line catalogs boast that they are open 24 hours a day for interested shoppers.

The producers of the Delia line of teen clothing and accessories have created an on-line catalog. Teens who visit Delia's web site have a chance to get free e-mail and the opportunity to build a home page. Discounts on Delia's products are offered for e-mail users who check their mail at this web site.

The advertising industry is betting on the success of on-line catalogs as a way to cash in on the revenue that the "wired generation" has. Keep an eye out for new advertising schemes that combine computer technology with sales. Even adults who are wary of making on-line purchases had better get ready to click their mouse!

FIGURE 2 (page 27) • 113

Reread the article, and circle all of the words that you do not already know. Then complete the following questions. In your answers, try to include as much detail as you can from your own experiences and from the information in the article.

1. What facts do you learn about teens in this article? Show this information as a web with words and, if you wish, drawings.

2. Explain what the author means by the term *wired generation*.

3. Will on-line shopping be an option that you will use? Why or why not?

CRITERIA REFERENCED ASSESSMENT OF ORAL LANGUAGE

	1	2	3	4	5
	Emerging	Beginning	Developing	Fluent	Proficient
Physical ■ voice ■ gesture ■ eye contact ■ nonverbal communication	little apparent control	limited control	some control	conscious use of voice and gesture	enhances communication
Language ■ word choice ■ arrangement of words	simple and repetitious	familiar and general	concrete and direct	clear, appropriate, and accurate	purposeful and flexible
Social ■ how individuals and groups relate together	largely unaware of others' needs	inconsistent	engaged	comfortable and responsive	shapes the way that the group works

FIGURE 5 (page 30) • 115

IN THE PRESENT

Language Structures:

_____ goes to school at _____.

_____ likes playing _____.

_____ likes _____.

_____ lives _____.

_____'s favorite _____ (color, movie, CD, TV show, singer) is

_____.

_____ goes to _____.

_____ is a _____ person.

Themes to build on include going to school, hobbies, living with others, favorite colors, friendship, worst nightmares, characteristics, television shows, movies, singers, reading books, family, and siblings.

IN THE PAST

Language Structures:

_____ was born in _____.

_____ moved to _____.

_____ visited _____.

_____ traveled to _____.

_____ went to school in _____.

_____ used to live in_____.

Themes to build on include birth place, previous schools attended, traveling, visiting, moving, and time.

IN THE FUTURE

Language Structures:

_____ wants to be _____.

_____ would like to save for _____.

_____ will be moving to _____.

_____ will go back to _____.

_____ will go to university to study _____.

_____ would like to marry _____.

_____ would like to be/have _____.

Themes to build on include career interests (e.g., fashion designer, paleontologist, animator, dentist), hopes (e.g., get married, make friends, save money to buy…), marks, things to learn (e.g., how to meet girls, swim).

Date:_____ Name: _____

ORAL READING ASSESSMENT

Practice reading the passage you have chosen, and then answer the following questions:

1. Why did you choose this passage?

2. What were you thinking about when you read this passage?

3. How does this passage relate to your own experiences?

4. What do you want me to notice as I listen to you read?

5. What do you do when you try to read a word that you do not know?

TEACHER NOTES:

Oral reading fluency:

| strong reader | competent reader | skills are developing (below grade level) |

Self correction strategies:

| used for errors that affect meaning | all errors are corrected | does not correct errors that affect meaning |

Speech difficulties:

Pronunciation difficulties:

Letter-sound associations:

Other observations:

FIGURE 7 (page 33) • **117**

ORAL ENGLISH LANGUAGE PROFICIENCY ASSESSMENT FOR KINDERGARTEN TO GRADE 3

Oral Interview and Activities

Name: _____

Date: _____

Initials of person who assessed the student:_____

Assessment Instructions:

- Ask the questions on the next page orally.

- Place a "check" where the student answers questions correctly.

- Write the student's *exact* response on the sheet.

- Place an *x* in spaces where the student is not capable of answering the question.

- Students with "advanced" English oral language skills will answer all of the questions correctly and relatively quickly. They may require support with the language of the classroom, which can be determined at a later date. "Intermediate" English language learners will answer more than one-third of the questions accurately. They may also require academic support and can be monitored over time in the classroom. "Beginners" will answer none or just a few of the questions. These students will require support immediately.

Scoring guide: responds accurately   ____ (√)

response incomplete   ____ (o)

no response   ____ (x)

This is an initial assessment only to help organize support for beginners. All further assessments should be curriculum-based within the context of authentic classroom tasks.

ESL ORAL ASSESSMENT: GRADES K-3

Oral Interview and Activities

1. What is your favorite food? Why is it your favorite food?

2. What is your favorite game? Why is it your favorite game?

3. Tell me about your family.

4. How high can you count? (Prompt if there is no response, and see if the learner continues.)

5. Tell me the names of these shapes. (Show a triangle, square, rectangle, and circle.)

6. Tell me the names of these body parts. (Point to two or three body parts.)

7. Tell me the names of these colors. (Show red, white, black, blue, yellow, and orange.)

8. Tell me the letters of the alphabet. (Prompt if there is no response, and see if the learner continues.)

9. What country are you from?

10. Ask me what my name is.

11. Ask me where the library is.

12. Ask me where the washroom is.

13. Pass me the book please.

14. What do you like to play at home?

15. Draw a picture of your home. Tell me about your home. (Prompt with questions.)

16. Draw a picture of your family. Tell me about your family. (Prompt with questions.)

17. Tell me about this picture. Show the student a photo or picture with a familiar scene.

Observation Notes: Write brief comments about anything unusual that may need to be monitored. For example, observations may be recorded about the student's speech (impediments, fluency, volume) or about body language (gestures, tics, confidence).

FIGURE 8 (CONT'D) • 119

ORAL ENGLISH LANGUAGE PROFICIENCY ASSESSMENT FOR GRADES 4 TO 9

Oral Interview and Activities

Name: _____

Date: _____

Initials of person who assessed the student:_____

Assessment Instructions:

- Ask the questions on the next page orally.

- Place a "check" where the student answers questions correctly.

- Write the student's *exact* response on the sheet.

- Place an *x* in spaces where the student is not capable of answering the question.

- Students with "advanced" English oral language skills will answer all of the questions correctly and relatively quickly. They may require support with the language of the classroom, which can be determined at a later date. "Intermediate" English language learners will answer more than one-third of the questions accurately. They may also require academic support and can be monitored over time in the classroom. "Beginners" will answer none or just a few of the questions. These students will require support immediately.

Scoring guide: responds accurately   ____ (√)

                   response incomplete   ____ (o)

                   no response   ____ (x)

This is an initial assessment only to help organize support for beginners. All further assessments should be curriculum-based within the context of authentic classroom tasks.

ESL ORAL ASSESSMENT: GRADES 4-9

Oral Interview and Activities

1. What are your first and last names?

2. How old are you?

3. When is your birthday?

4. Where do you live? What is your address/phone number?

5. What country did you come from? How long ago? Do you miss it?

6. Tell me three things about your last school. What did you study?

7. What did you do yesterday?

8. Tell me about some games or sports you like to play.

9. Ask me my name.

10. Ask me for a pencil.

11. Stand up, and touch your ear.

12. Sit down, and touch your nose.

13. Take the large red square, and put it under the small green triangle. (attributes)

14. Do you have a family (brother/sister/mother/father)? What are their names?

15. What is this called? (Point to various body parts.)

16. Describe the clothes that you are wearing.

17. Do you like to watch television? Tell me about something you have watched.

18. Draw a picture of your friend(s). What things do you like to do with your friends?

19. Tell me about this picture. (Show the student a photo or picture with a familiar scene.)

Observation Notes: Write brief comments about anything unusual that may need to be monitored. For example, observations may be recorded about the student's speech (impediments, fluency, volume) or about body language (gestures, tics, confidence).

FIGURE 9 (CONT'D) • 121

WRITTEN ENGLISH LANGUAGE PROFICIENCY ASSESSMENT FOR KINDERGARTEN TO GRADE 3

Writing Activities

Name: _____

Date: _____

Initials of person who assessed the student:_____

Assessment Instructions

- Read the directions aloud to the student (see next page).

- "Beginners" will write very little and/or will take a long time to start writing. Their writing may involve a few letters of the alphabet or words spelled phonetically. They may copy letters or words and may not generate them on their own. They may also illustrate their ideas instead of write them.

- "Advanced" learners will write relatively quickly. They will be able to use their writing to show meaning in simple sentences. There will be evidence of connections between sentences and of few errors.

- "Intermediate" learners will write somewhere between the range of beginners and advanced learners. There will be words that are repeated, one or two simple sentences, some accurate and some phonetic spelling.

- Suggested topics are included on page 123. Both narrative and expository (academic) writing are possible.

Scoring guide: **Beginning writer**   _____

Intermediate writer   _____

Advanced writer   _____

ESL WRITTEN ASSESSMENT, GRADES K-3

Directions:

Students will complete a writing sample to determine whether or not immediate ESL support and service is warranted. The writing will remain unedited and filed for future updating. This will establish a baseline for monitoring the development of writing over time.

Remember, this is just an initial assessment to give a baseline and to arrange immediate support for those students who need it. Beyond this, all writing assessments should be based on curriculum within the context of authentic classroom tasks.

1. Write four letters of the alphabet.

2. **Narrative Writing:** On a separate sheet of paper, write about a story you like.

3. **Academic Writing:** On a separate sheet of paper, write about an animal you like.

FIGURE 10 (CONT'D) • 123

WRITTEN ENGLISH LANGUAGE PROFICIENCY ASSESSMENT FOR GRADES 4-9

Writing Activities

Name: _____

Date: _____

Initials of person who assessed the student: _____

Assessment Instructions

- Read the topic aloud to the student. Encourage the student to make notes, draw, talk, or make a web to plan ideas before beginning to write.

- "Beginners" will write very little and/or will take a long time to start writing. Their narrative writing may not have a noticeable sequence of events. Writing will consist of phrases with grammatical errors, short sentences, and simple ideas.

- "Advanced" learners will write relatively quickly, may plan first using a web or notes, and will write sentences of some complexity with few errors. Writing will have a logical sequence and order with a noticeable beginning, middle, and end.

- "Intermediate" learners will write somewhere between the range of beginners and advanced learners. There may be a combination of phrases and sentences, some errors, evidence of some sequence and transition words/phrases.

- Suggested topics are included on page 125; both narrative and academic writing are possible.

Scoring guide: **Beginning writer** _____

                      Intermediate writer _____

                      Advanced writer _____

ESL WRITTEN ASSESSMENT, GRADES 4-9

Directions:

Students will complete a writing sample to determine if ESL support and service is warranted. The writing will remain unedited and be filed for future updating. This will establish a baseline for monitoring the development of writing over time.

Remember, this is just an initial assessment meant to give a baseline and to arrange immediate support for those students who need it. Beyond this, all writing assessments should be based on curriculum within the context of authentic classroom tasks.

Narrative Writing

Topic: A Story I Know

Write about a story that you know because someone has told it to you, you have told the story to someone, or you read the story at some time in your life. Include as many details as you remember.

Academic Writing

Topic: What I Know About Science or Another School Subject That I Like

Write about a school subject that you like such as science, math, language arts, or social studies. Give as many descriptive details as you can about what you study in the subject. Explain why you like the subject.

FIGURE 11 (CONT'D) • 125

ENGLISH LANGUAGE READING ASSESSMENT
FOR GRADES 4-9

Reading Comprehension Activities

Name: _____

Date: _____

Initials of person who assessed the student:_____

Directions:

- Select a story at the appropriate age/grade level. Have the student read the story aloud to you. When the student is finished, ask him/her to retell the story to you. Record his/her responses under appropriate headings on the Retelling Response Record: Story form.

  You may wish to photocopy a page of the chosen text, and record the student's oral reading performance. The following codes can be used:

  - omission   cat
  - repetition   cat
  - insertion   ∧
  - self corrects   SC
  - don't know   DK
  - reversal   the end
  - sounded out   SO

- Select a text of academic content at the appropriate age/grade level. Have the student read the text aloud to you. When the student is finished, ask him/her to retell the text and record his/her ideas on the Retelling Response Record: Information Text form.

- "Beginners" will be able to read isolated words, or they will read word by word. They will be able to repeat some words. Some beginners will only be able to describe the text from the drawings or pictures.

- "Intermediate" learners will retell some parts of the text. There will be evidence of decoding skills, and they will understand most of the meaning.

- "Advanced" learners will read relatively quickly and will retell most events and information accurately.

Note: Some teachers tape-record this informal assessment to make scoring easier.

Scoring guide: **Beginning reader** _____

Intermediate reader _____

Advanced reader _____

Students who experience great difficulty reading basic material will require intensive support immediately.

Remember, this initial assessment provides a baseline and enables you to arrange immediate support for students who need it. Beyond this, all assessments should be based on curriculum within the context of authentic classroom tasks.

FIGURE 12 (CONT'D) • 127

Name: _____ Grade: _____ Text: _____

Retelling Response Record: Story

Student's summary of the main idea or theme of the story.

Supporting ideas given by the student.

Student's description about the:

- Characters

- Setting

- Action

- Information that was/was not sequenced appropriately.

- Additional information volunteered when comprehension questions were asked (who, what, where, when, why, how).

Other comments about the retelling:

Name: _____ Grade: _____ Text: _____

Retelling Response Record: Information Text

Student's summary of the main idea or theme of the story.

Supporting ideas given by the student.

Student's description about the:

- Main idea

- Relationship of the main idea to the meaning

- Details recalled

- Predictions made about meaning of the text

- Additional information volunteered when comprehension questions were asked (who, what, where, when, why, how). Relationship of student's own experiences to the information.

Other comments about the retelling:

FIGURE 14 (page 38) • 129

INFORMAL DESCRIPTORS OF READING PROFICIENCY IN ENGLISH

FOCUS	BEGINNING/ EMERGING	BEGINNING	INTERMEDIATE/ DEVELOPING	INTERMEDIATE/ EXPANDING	ADVANCED/ PROFICIENT
Reading ■ narrative or literary ■ core academic content or expository	■ virtually no proficiency in reading in English ■ listens to stories read aloud ■ can repeat some words ■ recognizes sound/symbol relationships ■ shows an awareness of print ■ shows an awareness that words have meaning	■ beginner reader English ■ can follow along with choral reading ■ can retell some parts of simple narrative texts ■ uses some phonics and/or other decoding skills ■ reads simple descriptive lesson material	■ reads basic, simple reading material in English ■ retells the beginning, middle, and end of most stories ■ recognizes plot, character, and the main story events ■ reads and understands some simple content/ expository text material in core academic subject areas ■ makes regular use of the dictionary to seek word meanings	■ expanding reading ability to include some content material in English ■ reads some narrative material independently ■ recognizes setting, character, plot, climax, conflict, and resolution in most stories ■ can read orally ■ has awareness of the meaning conveyed in poetry ■ can predict content and read between the lines sometimes and make inferences ■ comprehension of content vocabulary in core academic subject areas is expanding	■ reads and understands general academic material in English ■ reads and understands general narrative and expository material ■ relates reading to experiences ■ uses a variety of reading strategies ■ recognizes literary elements and genres ■ can extract important details from text ■ still reads below native-English speed and sometimes needs to use dictionary to aid comprehension ■ timed tests present some problems

INFORMAL DESCRIPTORS OF WRITING PROFICIENCY IN ENGLISH

FOCUS	BEGINNING/ EMERGING	BEGINNING	INTERMEDIATE/ DEVELOPING	INTERMEDIATE/ EXPANDING	ADVANCED/ PROFICIENT
Writing • narrative or literary • core academic content or expository	• virtually no proficiency in writing in English • writes letters or single, simple words • copies letters and simple words from a model • exhibits little awareness of spelling, capitalization, or punctuation	• beginner writer in English • writes or copies phrases and patterned, simple sentences • uses limited and repetitious vocabulary in writing samples • uses phonetic spelling • makes frequent errors in structure and spelling, obscuring meaning • writes very slowly	• writes basic, simple sentences in English • writes simple sentences in the present tense • has trouble with subject-verb agreement in writing • run-on sentences are common structures in writing • uses high-frequency words • has some difficulty with word order • often omits endings and/or words • uses some capitalization, punctuation, and transitional spelling • errors frequently interfere with meaning • little understanding of paragraph organization • writes simple sentences about academic content but cannot collect information and write in detail	• expanding ability to write in literary and academic subject areas in English • able to write a simple paragraph with little elaboration of ideas • writing exhibits inconsistent use of a variety of verb tenses, subject-verb agreement, and other errors • limited use of transition words, articles, prepositions, and descriptive details • uses punctuation, capitalization, and conventional spelling but continues to make some errors that interfere with comprehension • has difficulty with written material under timed or test conditions • does not understand idioms • shows little ability to write expository/ argumentative material/essays	• writes well both literary and academic/narrative and academic/expository • able to coherently connect more than one paragraph • can elaborate on ideas • is able to present a main idea with supporting details • uses appropriate verb tenses most of the time • errors in sentence structure do not interfere with meaning • uses varied vocabulary that is appropriate for different styles/purposes • very few errors in mechanics – capitalization, punctuation, or spelling • writes with some errors in idioms • speed is improving but still writes below the speed of native-English writers

FIGURE 16 (page 40) • 131

INFORMAL DESCRIPTORS OF ORAL LANGUAGE PROFICIENCY IN ENGLISH: SPEAKING AND LISTENING

FOCUS	BEGINNING/EMERGING	BEGINNING	INTERMEDIATE/DEVELOPING	INTERMEDIATE/EXPANDING	ADVANCED/PROFICIENT
1. Speaking	■ virtually no English speaking proficiency	■ begins to communicate personal and survival needs	■ asks and answers questions about personal needs and familiar simple topics	■ converses intelligibly in most social situations but academic conversations are challenging	■ participates effectively in both social and academic conversations with only occasional idiomatic difficulties
(a) Fluency	■ repeats an occasional word(s) ■ speech is halting and fragmented ■ limited or no social or classroom conversation ■ virtually no knowledge of English sentence structures	■ frequent basic errors ■ uses one word utterances and short patterns or phrases in social conversation ■ usually hesitant and sometimes silenced by language limitations in the classroom	■ speaks hesitantly, often rephrasing and searching for words and/or the correct manner of expression ■ speech is better in everyday conversations than in classroom discussions	■ speaks with occasional hesitation ■ speech is generally fluent with occasional lapses while seeking appropriate expressions in classroom discussions	■ speaks with near-native fluency — hesitations do not interfere with most communication ■ speech in both everyday conversations and classroom discussions is relatively effortless
(b) Structure	■ virtually no English vocabulary	■ many errors in grammar and order ■ must rephrase often	■ uses mainly present tense verbs ■ omits words and endings often ■ frequent errors of grammar and word order	■ uses some sentence variety ■ inconsistency in applying rules of grammar ■ some errors in word order, endings	■ grammatical usage and word order approximate that of a native-English speaker
(c) Vocabulary		■ uses functional vocabulary ■ vocabulary is limited ■ frequent misuse of words	■ uses limited vocabulary ■ conversation limited by lack of vocabulary in social and classroom discussions	■ uses adequate vocabulary ■ few word usage errors ■ conversation in social situations is adequate ■ limited classroom conversation	■ use of vocabulary and idioms approximates that of a native-English speaker in conversations, in social situations, and in the classroom ■ uses varied vocabulary

INFORMAL DESCRIPTORS OF ORAL LANGUAGE PROFICIENCY IN ENGLISH (CONT'D)

FOCUS	BEGINNING/EMERGING	BEGINNING	INTERMEDIATE/DEVELOPING	INTERMEDIATE/EXPANDING	ADVANCED/PROFICIENT
2. Listening Aural Comprehension	■ understands virtually no English conversation ■ does not understand most English words and phrases ■ has a beginner's understanding of a few letters and sounds in English	■ begins to understand words and phrases in conversations that help meet personal and survival needs ■ understands a few English words and phrases but only if spoken slowly ■ requires frequent repetition ■ has difficulty following conversations of any length ■ has difficulty following the sequence of simple directions ■ can only recall and retell a few events in a story	■ understands and answers questions in conversations ■ familiar experiences and topics are the main focus of comprehension ■ can follow simple social conversations when the topics are familiar ■ understands most of what is said if it is spoken slowly ■ following classroom directions is difficult ■ does not understand conversations about most academic subject matter or content	■ understands conversation in most social situations but academic understanding presents difficulty ■ understands most social conversations at normal speed ■ understands most classroom discussions and uses requests for repetition, rephrasing, and clarification to support comprehension ■ has difficulty understanding conversations about academic subject content	■ understands both social and academic conversations with only occasional idiomatic difficulties ■ understands most social conversations at normal speed, both in and out of the classroom ■ can recall and retell most information heard in an appropriate sequence ■ understands most discussions of academic content in subject classes

FIGURE 17 (CONT'D) • 133

STUDENT-LED CONFERENCE FORM: GRADES K-3

Name: _____   Date: _____

A drawing and/or words that show the work that I am proud of:

A drawing and/or words that show something I am trying to change:

A drawing and/or words that show my goals:

For Friends	For School Work	For Myself

STUDENT-LED CONFERENCE FORM: GRADES 4-9

Name: _____   Date: _____

Work that I am proud of:

_____

_____

_____

_____

_____

Some things I know I need to work on:

_____

_____

_____

_____

Three goals for next term

Social: _____

_____

_____

_____

Academic: _____

_____

_____

Personal: _____

_____

_____

_____

FIGURE 19 (page 47) • 135

PARENTS' COMMENTS

What I am proud of:

_____

_____

_____

_____

_____

_____

How I will support your learning:

_____

_____

_____

_____

_____

_____

Student's signature: _____

Parent's signature: _____

TEN THINGS PARENTS CAN DO AT HOME TO SUPPORT THE LEARNING OF ESL STUDENTS, GRADES K-3

1. Visit the local library on a regular basis. Ensure your child has a library card and is able to use it. Accompany your child for story times at the library.

2. Set aside at least fifteen minutes a day for family reading. Read to your child in English and/or in the language of the home, and listen to your child read. Read both stories and information books about people, places, things, and events. Talk about who is in the pictures, where they are, what is happening, why it is happening, and make predictions about what will happen next.

3. Visit places in the community with your child to encourage new interests. These places can be the beach, the woods, a science center, museums, art galleries, and anything else your community has to offer.

4. Take an interest in writing by having your child draw and talk to you about what he/she has created. Write a description of the drawing for your child in English and/or in the language of the home.

5. Together, explore the print in magazine and newspapers, on signs, and in the community at large.

6. Create a place within the home that is quiet and free from distractions where your child can do school work.

7. Keep a scrapbook of your child's work so he/she knows that you value what is being done. Provide your child with positive feedback about his/her progress in learning.

8. Support your child's developing bilingualism. He/she is not replacing the language of the home with English. Your child is becoming bilingual. Studies show that those with command of both English and the language of the home are, in the long term, more likely to have success as a learner.

9. Attend parent-teacher conferences, and ask for a translator if you need one.

10. Become involved in your child's school, if possible, by helping out with school activities such as field trips and other school events.

FIGURE 21 (page 49) • **137**

TEN THINGS PARENTS CAN DO AT HOME TO SUPPORT THE LEARNING OF ESL STUDENTS, GRADES 4-9

1. With your child, visit the local library on a regular basis. Ensure your child has a library card and is able to use it.

2. Set aside at least twenty minutes a day for family reading. Encourage your child to read novels (in any language) and a variety of information books about people, places, things, and events from the past, present, and future. Read books with geographical maps, drawings and sketches, diagrams, charts, graphs, or photographs.

3. Together, visit places in the community to encourage your child to develop new interests. Some suggestions are the beach, the woods, a science center, museums, and art galleries. Ask your child to tell you what he/she is learning at school.

4. Take an interest in writing by having your child write in a private diary or journal, or by writing to friends and family at home. Encourage your child to experiment with different forms of writing: poems, information, stories, lists, flow charts, letters of persuasion.

5. Create a place within the home that is quiet and free from distractions where your child can do school work

6. Help your son/daughter to get organized. Set up a daily schedule with a routine work/study time, and monitor homework. Offer positive support and suggestions as needed.

7. Help your child learn strategies for managing the information in textbooks and for note-taking. Find books in the library on study skills, enrol your child in a mini-course, or ask teachers or the teacher-librarian at your child's school for ideas.

8. If you can afford to hire a tutor, ask the tutor to help your child develop note-taking skills, strategies for learning, and study skills. In addition to working on classroom assignments, some of the time with the tutor should be used to "learn how to learn."

9. Monitor the amount of time your son/daughter spends on games on the computer, on chat-lines, and on e-mail.

10. Be positive and supportive. Balance time for study with time for play. Learning should be something that brings pleasure, not a chore that takes away from free time: ensure your child has time for activities other than the formal learning of English. Keep in mind that much language acquisition occurs in social situations.

FIGURE 23 (page 61) • 139

FIGURE 23 (CONT'D) • 141

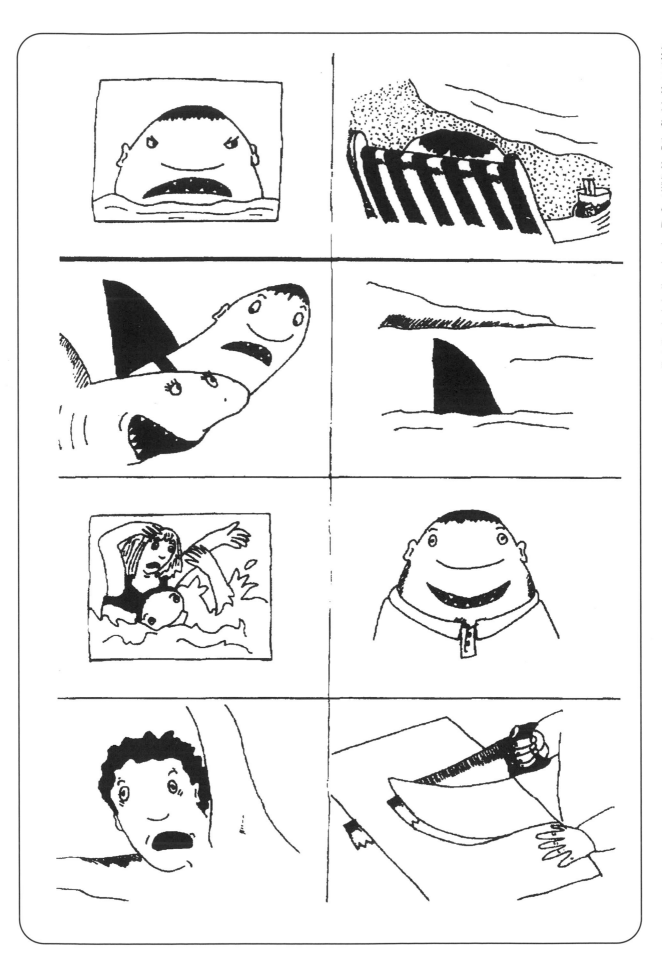

Characters	Setting ■ place ■ time of day or season
A Surprising Event	An Object
A Problem for the Characters	Solving the Problem

FIGURE 25 (page 65) • 143

MY THINKING

Pictures in my head	Words or phrases I heard
Questions I have	My feelings

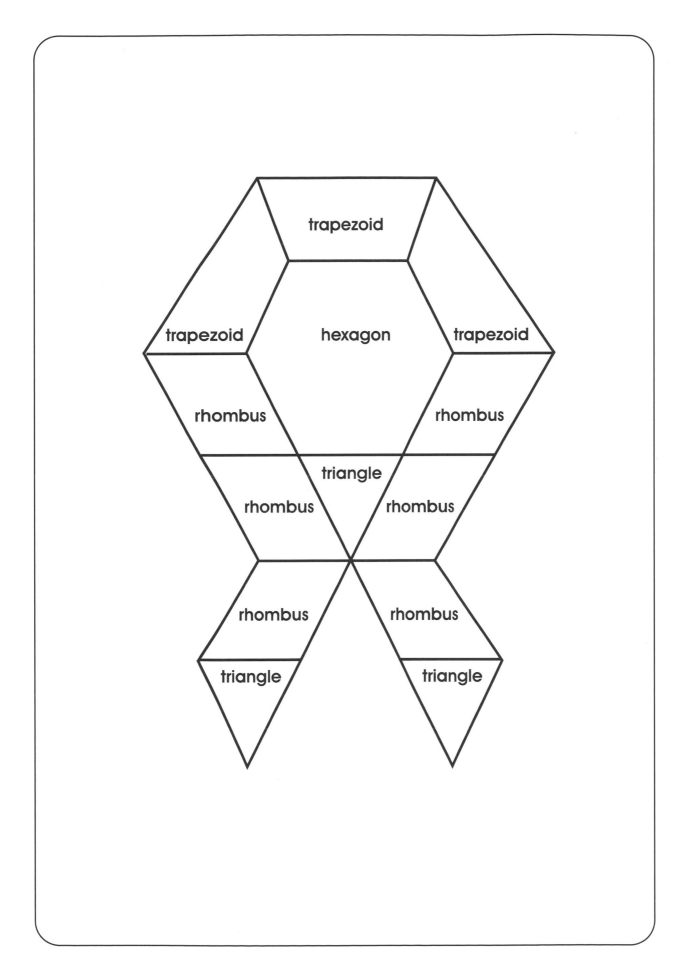

FIGURE 32 (page 71) • 145

THINKING LIKE AN ARCHAEOLOGIST

Look carefully at the object to determine:

- size, color, and weight
- materials it is made from
- way it was made
- any decoration on the object
- if it is ancient or modern

Uses:

- Possible uses of the object: for cooking, decoration, hunting, fishing, farming; for working, making music, religious purposes; as furniture; and so on
- Who might have used it? (e.g., farmers, city dwellers, artists, soldiers, students)
- Is such an object used today? Do you know of an object we use today that is similar?

Lifestyles:

- Would children, women, men, or the elderly have used this object?
- Where was it used? (e.g., indoors, rural or urban areas, outdoors)
- What might the object tell us about the lives of the people who used it? (e.g., work, leisure time, interests)
- What kind of people?
- Is it ancient or modern?

Based on our observations and discussion of this artifact, we believe that the

artifact might have been used for: _____

by the _____ people.

Name: _____

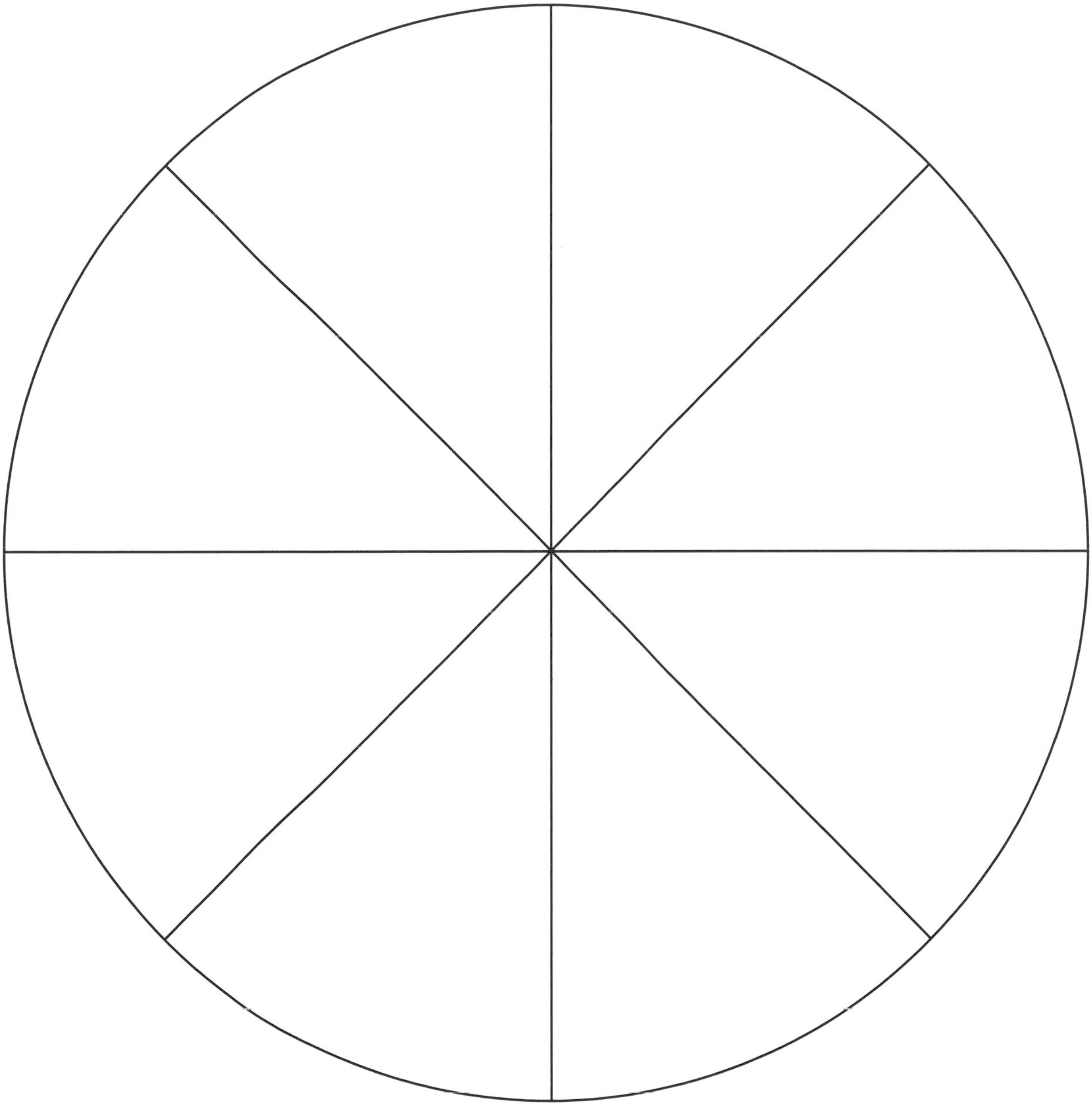

FIGURE 37 (page 88) • **147**

Group members: _____

Our story title: _____

Work with your group to get ideas from photos and your story to help you fill in this chart. Use drawings and words to explain your thinking.

Country:

Climate/Geographical Information:

Cultural Information (festivals, religious beliefs):

Other Information (clothing, food, language, animals):

MULTICULTURAL CINDERELLA PLAYS

Name: _____

One thing I noticed about each play:

a. _____

_____

b. _____

_____

c. _____

_____

d. _____

_____

e. _____

_____

Cultural Information included in our play

Country: _____

Customs: _____

_____

_____

_____

FIGURE 40 (page 92) • **149**

THE ENCHANTED ANKLET

Setting: Cindurinagar, India

Characters: Cinduri, Stepmother, Stepsister, Prince, Godfather Snake

Narrator: Cinduri's parents died so she was left to depend on her stepmother.
                 Her stepmother makes Cinduri go to the lake to get water. Cinduri
                 must also cook, get vegetables, and do many other chores.

Stepmother: Do your chores now Cinduri!

Cenduri: Yes, stepmother. Whatever you say.

Stepsister: Wash my dresses.

Stepmother: Did you do your chores?

Cinduri: Yes, stepmother, all of my chores are done.

Narrator: One day when Cinduri is at the lake gathering water, she sees a snake
                 with a jewel on its head.

Godfather: I will be your Godfather for ever.

Cinduri: Thank you very, very much. That's wonderful.

Stepmother: We are going to the Navaratri Festival but you cannot go. You have to
                 do your work on the farm.

Narrator: Cinduri is disappointed so she goes to find her Godfather snake.

Cinduri: Please help me go to the festival.

Godfather: Take this jewel. Rub the jewel and make a wish. (She rubs the jewel.)

Narrator: Cinduri's old rags magically turned into a beautiful sari. She went to
                 the festival and there everyone thought that she was beautiful.

Prince: Would you dance with me?

Cinduri: Of course your highness. I'd be honored.

Narrator: Cinduri had to leave the festival early and she lost the anklet on the
                 doorstep.

Prince: Wait! How will I find you? I don't even know your name. (The prince
                 picks up the anklet.)

Prince: I will find the girl who owns this anklet. Whoever fits the anklet is
                 the girl whom I will marry.

Narrator: Many young women try on the anklet but it does not fit them, The
                 prince finally arrives at Cinduri's house.

Prince: I want you girls to try on this anklet. (The stepsister tries on the
                 anklet but it doesn't fit.)

Prince: (speaking to Cinduri) Would you like to try on the anklet?

Cinduri: Of course I would your highness.

Narrator: Cinduri tried on the anklet and it fit perfectly. The Prince and
                 Cinduri were married that very day.

INDIVIDUAL NOVEL STUDY

Name: _____

Grade: _____

Date: _____

Title of novel:

_____

Author:

_____

Type of novel (for example, fiction, adventure):

_____

My predictions about the novel – I think this story is about:

Consider who, where, what, why, when, and how.

Character

Read chapter __. After you have read the chapter, do the following:

1. Choose one interesting character or animal from the chapter.

2. Make a web to help you organize details in the novel about the character or animal.

3. In your own words, using the notes collected on your web, write a description of the character.

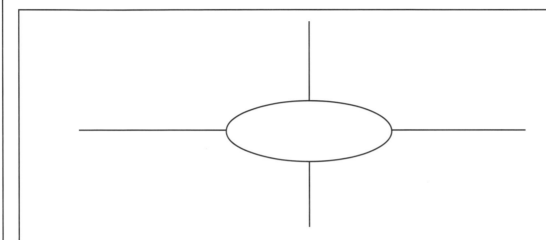

Add your own categories such as: physical appearance, character, interests and hobbies, jobs, or living arrangements.

Description of _____(character's name)

_____

_____

_____

_____

_____

_____

_____

Use words that will help you write your description; for example: *a, an, the, to be, have, see, feel, weigh, hear, look, appear, who, which, him, her, he, she, it, thin, slender, big, small, round, green, tall,* or *short.*

Setting

Draw the setting (place, location, or scene that interests you) from chapter __.
Then, write to describe the setting you have illustrated. Be sure to include details
in your writing.

Drawing of the setting in chapter __.

Description of _____ (setting, place, location, scene):

_____

_____

_____

_____

_____

_____

_____

Use words that will help you write your description; for example: *a, an, the, to be, have,
see, feel, weigh, hear, look, appear, who, which, him, her, he, she, it, thin, slender, big, small,
round, green, tall,* or *short.*

Time Line

Organize the important events in chapter __ in a sequence on the time line from the beginning of the action to the end of the action. Then, use your time line to write the events in the order that they occurred.

Put the action in time order.

Sequence of events or actions in _____ chapters:

_____

_____

_____

_____

_____

_____

_____

Use sequence and transition words to help you write about the events; for example: *first, in the beginning, initially, to start, then, next, second, third, last, after, finally, at the end, in conclusion, in summary, at, beside, above/below, over/under, next to, between, in front of,* or *behind.*

Illustrated Action Strip

1. Choose several scenes from your time line.

2. Decide which scene represents the problem, the climax or most important moment, and the resolution or the way the problem was solved.

3. Illustrate each scene with drawings and words.

Scenes

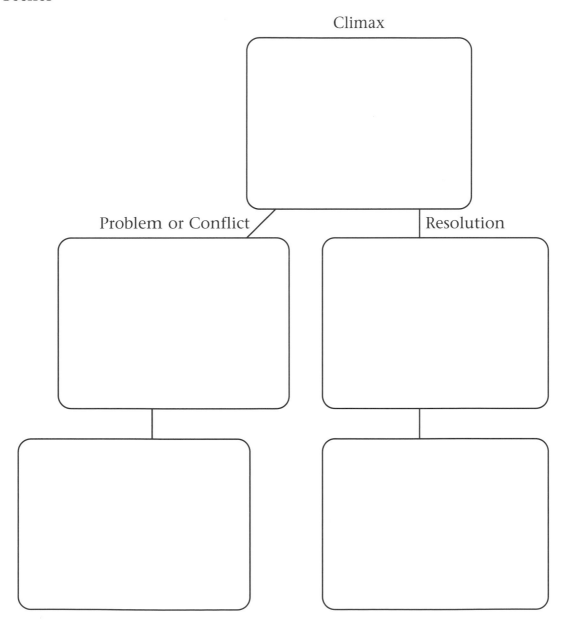

Use language of action/consequences/reaction to help you; for example: *is caused by, is the result of, is a consequence of, because, is probably, most likely, predict, forecast,* or *if/then.*

Choosing and Decision Making

1. Write about or illustrate the problem or conflict in the novel.

2. Write about or illustrate the resolution to the problem.

3. On a decision-making diagram, organize the choices the character made and another option.

Problem and/or conflict in the novel:

Choices and decisions made by the characters to resolve the conflict or problem:

Decision-Making Diagram

decision or choice

problem or conflict

decision or choice

Use language that will help you write about choices; for example: *can, will, may, might, could, to decide, to choose, to take,* or *to select.*

Evaluating the Novel

1. Add categories that were important in the novel you have read for evaluation.

2. Complete the chart.

3. Use the information you have organized to write an evaluation of the novel.

Categories	Rating Scale						
add your own	Very Poor	Poor	Satisfactory	Good	Very Good	Excellent	Outstanding
	1	2	3	4	5	6	7
setting							
main character							
plot							
conflict							
resolution							

Evaluation of the novel: _____

_____

_____

_____

_____

_____

_____

Use words that help you write your evaluation; for example: *to rank, to evaluate, to believe, to value, to analyze, good/better/best, satisfactory/unsatisfactory, right/wrong,* or *good/evil.*

INVESTIGATING A CURRENT STORY IN THE NEWS

Choose an ongoing story in the news and collect all the articles and information that you can find on that topic. You will need a minimum of five different articles. Record the date of each article and the source in which the article was found. For those of you who are able to read newspapers or magazines in a language other than English, include a short translation of the main ideas in the article.

The key will be to choose a topic that interests you. You will be reading newspapers and magazines for several weeks to gather information about your topic. Before you start to collect articles, you must see me to approve your topic.

Remember, this is an ongoing assignment, and it cannot be completed in a few days.

You will be evaluated on the following components:

1. Organization of the articles as outlined above.

2. A summary of the articles written as an expository essay (a detailed outline will be provided for you to follow).

3. Your conclusions, based on what you have read on your chosen topic.

INVESTIGATING A CURRENT STORY IN THE NEWS: ESSAY OUTLINE

After you have collected news articles on your topic, reread each article and highlight ideas that you have identified as being important. Follow this outline for the paragraphs required in the essay.

(a) Paragraph 1

- introductory paragraph: introduces the reader to your topic and to the *three subtopics* to be discussed in the essay

(b) Paragraph 2

- introductory sentence: the first subtopic (explain this in detail)
- include an example from your news articles that gives more information about the subtopic (a quotation from the article could be used as a supporting statement)
- explain your example clearly

(c) Paragraph 3

- introductory sentence: the second subtopic
- use an example from one of the articles
- explain your example clearly

(d) Paragraph 4

- introductory sentence: the third subtopic
- use an example from one of the articles
- explain your example clearly

(e) Paragraph 5

- include the central ideas from paragraphs 2 through 4
- include the consequences of your findings
- include your predictions for the future

The final draft of the essay should be approximately one page in length.

FIGURE 44 (page 100) • 159

NEWS ESSAY SELF-EVALUATION SHEET

Reread your essay for the purpose of self-evaluation. Give yourself marks for including the following components:

Introduction/Paragraph 1

- explanation of the new story in an introductory sentence /1 mark
- the three subtopics in the essay are introduced /1 mark

Paragraph 2

- the first subtopic is included /1 mark
- one example is given explaining the subtopic /1 mark
- one quote or reference is included /1 mark

Paragraph 3

- the second subtopic is included /1 mark
- one example is given explaining the subtopic /1 mark
- one quote or reference is included /1 mark

Paragraph 4

- the third subtopic is included /1 mark
- one example is given explaining the subtopic /1 mark
- one quote or reference is included /1 mark

Paragraph 5

- a concluding statement about the topic is included /1 mark
- a summary of the main points is made /1 mark
- a statement about future considerations is included /1 mark

Once you have completed the self-evaluation, exchange essays and evaluation sheets with a partner to check that you are both in agreement with the marks given for each other's essay. Try to reach a consensus about the mark. Your signatures will indicate that both of you agreed with the mark given for this essay.

Essay mark /14   Signature: _____
(student)   author

Essay mark /14   Signature: _____
(teacher)   reader

ANNOTATED
BIBLIOGRAPHY

Ashworth, M. *Effective Teachers, Effective Schools: Second-Language Teaching in Australia, Canada, England and the United States.* Toronto: Pippin, 2000.

- provides an account of the history, policy, laws, and evolution of ESL practices across countries

- presents solid, basic information concerning effective practices for ESL teachers and for developing programs and curricula from a theoretical perspective

Ashworth, M., and P. Wakefield. *Teaching the World's Children: ESL for Ages Three to Seven.* Toronto: Pippin, 1994.

- provides basic information about learning ESL in the early years

- topics include the role of language in learning and literacy, establishing learning centers, building cultural bridges, and considering the community

British Columbia Ministry of Education. *Enhancing Group Communication Skills Across Curriculum.* Victoria, BC: British Columbia Ministry of Education, 1995.

- provides a concise set of descriptions of five phases of development in group communication skills, measured against five attributes of group communication skills

- accompanying videotape of classroom lessons and rubric of descriptions

Brownlie, F., and J. King. *Learning in Safe Schools: Creating Classrooms Where All Children Belong.* Markham, ON: Pembroke Publishers, 2000.

- encourages schools to build cultures that include all students

- offers many practical strategies such as school-wide code of conduct, lesson planning, building resource teams, and learning journeys

Brownlie, F. and C. Feniak. *Student Diversity: Addressing the Needs of All Learners in Inclusive Classrooms*. Markham, ON: Pembroke Publishers, 1999.

- presents practical lessons and strategies for working in inclusive schools and for supporting the achievements of all learners

- presents ideas for reading assessments within classroom contexts

- strategies have been field-tested by practicing classroom teachers

Brownlie, F., and S. Close. *Beyond Chalk and Talk: Collaborative Strategies for the Middle and High School Years.* Markham, ON: Pembroke Publishers, 1992.

- presents case studies that involve students in collaborative learning as they acquire hands-on experience with problem solving in the content areas

- strategies have been field-tested by classroom teachers

Brownlie, F., S. Close, and L. Wingren. *Tomorrow's Classroom Today: Strategies for Creating Active Readers, Writers, and Thinkers*. Markham, ON: Pembroke Publishers, 1990.

- classroom-tested strategies for active, collaborative learning

Brownlie, F., S. Close, and L. Wingren. *Reaching for Higher Thought: Reading, Writing, Thinking Strategies*. Edmonton: Arnold Publishing, 1988.

- classroom-tested strategies to support the learning of all students

Cummins, J. "Language assessment and academic achievement." In J. W. Ollier (ed.), *Issues in Language Testing Research*. Rowley, MA: Newbury House, 1983.

- discusses the need to pay greater attention to classroom-based assessment of student performance in order to support the continuing academic achievements of bilingual students at school

- explains how high expectations for ESL students help them become fully and fluently bilingual both to communicate and to achieve at school.

Cummins, J. "Language and literacy acquisition in bilingual contexts." In *Journal of Multilingual & Multicultural Development* , 10, 1, 1989: 17-51.

- explains how proficiency in a first language can promote proficiency in the second language

- supports the development of school-based language policies and decisions regarding bilingualism

DeBoer, A., and S. Fister. *Working Together: Tools for Collaborative Teaching.* Longmont, CO: Soporis West, 1997.

- gives strategies and practices for working effectively in a resource team model and/or for working collaboratively as a resource person with classroom teachers

- provides practical and effective techniques; some black line masters

Gibbons, P. *Learning to Learn in a Second Language.* Portsmouth, NH: Heinemann, 1991.

- excellent and practical book that gives basic information concerning English second-language learning, cultural adjustment and reasons for the teaching, and assessment of reading and writing

- presents practical strategies for oral language teaching and assessment as well as for the teaching and assessment of reading and writing

- provides ideas for language and content instruction, which is its primary focus, but has intermediate applications

Hagan, J., et al. *The Speech and Language Classroom Intervention Manual.* Columbia, MO: Hawthorne Educational Services, 1990.

- provides strategies for speech and language intervention with learners who are experiencing difficulty

- supports the teacher in changing practice before referring learners for diagnostic services

Irujo, S. *Teaching Bilingual Children: Beliefs and Behaviors.* Boston: Heinle & Heinle Publishers, 1998.

- provides teacher discussion about ways of teaching bilingual children and the reasons for doing so

- progressive discussion of bilingual education from the point of view of being an asset to child development rather than a deficit

- addresses issues of learning, language learning, culture and classroom organization

McCarney, S., and J. Tucci. *Study Skills for Students in Our Schools.* Columbia, MO: Hawthorne Educational Services, 1990.

- gives strategies for encouraging students to develop effective study skills

- provides a list of interventions for learners who are experiencing difficulty understanding or "doing" school

Mohan, B. *Language and Content*. Reading, MA: Addison-Wesley, 1986.

- gives the theoretical rationale for teaching language through content

- presents ways of organizing lessons for teaching language more effectively than it has traditionally been taught in isolation of content

- provides a framework for organizing content lessons that also teach language

- presents excellent discussion of cultural bias in assessment

Mohan, B., C. Leung, and C. Davison (eds.). *English as a Second Language in the Mainstream: Teaching Learning and Identity*. Essex, England: Pearson Educational, 2001.

- gives an account of the teaching of ESL learners in Australia, England, and Canada

- excellent discussion of the need to coordinate language learning with the learning of curricular content

- demonstrates how to use graphic organizers effectively and why explicit teaching of how to use them is so important

- argues for support for ESL learners within education since they are in many places in the mainstream

O'Malley, J., and L. Pierce. *Authentic Assessment for English Language Learners: Practical Applications for Teachers*. Reading, MA: Addison-Wesley, 1996.

- includes excellent discussion of how to make the assessment of ESL learners more authentic by housing it within the context of classroom activities

- provides a synopsis of research in the area

- uses rubrics and strategies for reading, writing, and oral language assessment – makes suggestions for content area assessment

- presents a good discussion of how to develop portfolios

O'Malley, M., and A. U. Chamot. *The CALLA Handbook. Implementing the Cognitive Academic Language Learning Approach*. New York: Addison-Wesley, 1994.

- provides strategies for teaching ESL students in the content areas (science, social studies, math, and so on) in the upper intermediate grades

- combines language learning and content area instruction effectively

Short, D., et al. *ESL Standards for Pre-K-12 Students.* Alexandria, VA: Teachers of English to Speakers of Other Languages (TESOL), 1997.

- includes goals and standards for aligning curriculum content with social and academic: language learning and socio-cultural objectives

- encourages the teaching of language, culture, and content

- provides practical, concise statements and principles for effective practices

- presents excellent discussion of language learning/teaching

Spangenberg-Urbschat, K., and R. Pritchard (eds.). *Kids Come in All Languages: Reading Instruction for ESL Students.* Newark, DL: International Reading Association (IRA), 1994.

- provides excellent and succinct discussion of the ramifications of failing to adequately address the needs of culturally and linguistically diverse student populations in school districts with diverse student populations

- discusses the relationship between self-esteem and learning, the importance of honoring students' home languages, cultures and ethnicity for learning

- gives an overview of teaching and instructional approaches that are effective in meeting the needs of ESL students

- emphasizes the importance of learning the academic content areas of the curriculum rather than only providing a simple and superficial understanding of language in isolation of this content

Swartz, R., and S. Parks. *Infusing Critical and Creative Thinking into Content Instruction: A Lesson Design Handbook for the Elementary Grades.* Pacific Grove, CA: Critical Thinking Press, 1994.

- very practical classroom guide for teaching language and content through the use of graphic organizers with text

- includes black line masters and sample lessons across subject areas

Thomas, W. P., and V. Collier. *School Effectiveness for Language Minority Students.* Washington, DC: National Clearinghouse for Bilingual Education, 1997.

- based on a study of 700,000 ESL learners who were followed through school for ten years

- gives contemporary research in English second-language instruction

- compares/contrasts various program models and the development of language learning within these models

- makes recommendations for effective educational practices

CHILDREN'S LITERATURE

Adams, E. B. (ed.) *Korean Cinderella*. Seoul, South Korea: Seoul International Publishing House, 1989.

Caburn, J.R. *Angkat: The Cambodian Cinderella*. Auburn, CA: Shen's Books, 1998.

Climo, S. *The Egyptian Cinderella*. New York: HarperCollins, 1989.

_____. *The Irish Cinderella*. New York: HarperCollins, 1996.

_____. *The Korean Cinderella*. New York: HarperCollins, 1993.

_____. *The Persian Cinderella*. New York: HarperCollins, 1999.

Coerr, Eleanor. *Sadako*. New York: G. P. Putnam's Sons, 1993.

de las Paz, M. *Abedeha: The Philippine Cinderella*. CA: Pacific Queen Communications, 1991.

Goble, Paul. *Beyond the Ridge*. New York: Bradbury Press, 1989.

Hooks, W. H. *Moss Gown*. New York: Clarion Books, 1987.

Jacobs, J. (ed.) *Tattercoats*. New York: G. P. Putnam's Sons, 1989.

Louie, A. *Yeh-Shen*. New York: Philomel Books, 1982.

Mahy, M. *The Great White Man-Eating Shark*. Markham, ON: Penguin Books, 1989.

Martin, R., and D. Shannon. *The Rough Face Girl*. New York: G. P. Putnam's Sons, 1992.

Mehta, L. *The Enchanted Anklet*. Toronto: Limur Publishing, 1985.

Phulma. *Nomi and the Magic Fish*. New York: Doubleday, 1972.

San Souci, R. *The Talking Eggs*. New York: Dial Books for Young Readers, 1989.

Scieszka, Jon. *The True Story of the Three Little Pigs*. New York: Scholastic, 1989.

Schoenherr, John. *Bear*. New York: Philomel Books, 1991.

Steptoe, J. *Mufaro's Beautiful Daughters: An African Tale*. New York: Lothrop, Lee & Shepard, 1987.

Vuong, L. D. *The Brocaded Slipper*. Reading, MA: Addison-Wesley, 1982.

Wallace, Ian. 1984. *Chin Chiang and the Dragon's Dance*. Vancouver, BC: Douglas & McIntyre, 1984.

Whitney, T. *Vasilia the Beautiful*. New York: The Macmillan Co., 1970.

Wise, W. *The Black Falcon*. New York: Philomel Books, 1990.

Young, Ed. 1989. *Lon Po Po*. New York: Scholastic, 1989.

ONLINE REFERENCES

Teachers of English to Speakers of Other Languages (TESOL)
www.tesol.edu/index.htm

or

www.tesol.edu/pubs/index.html (publications index)

- includes articles and papers, publications, and links to other sites

National Clearinghouse for Bilingual Education
www.rncbe.gwu.edu/

- includes articles and papers, publications, and links to other sites

www.bctf.bc.ca/ESL/

- includes links to other sites and lessons